Meaningful Phy $

This book outlines an approach to teaching and learning in physical education that prioritises meaningful experiences for pupils, using case studies to illustrate how practitioners have implemented this approach across international contexts.

Prioritising the idea of meaningfulness positions movement as a primary way to enrich the quality of young people's lives, shifting the focus of physical education programs to better suit the needs of contemporary young learners and resist the utilitarian health-oriented views of physical education that currently predominate in many schools and policy documents. The book draws on the philosophy of physical education to articulate the main rationale for prioritising meaningful experiences before identifying potential and desired outcomes for participants. It highlights the distinct characteristics of Meaningful physical education and its content, and outlines teaching and learning principles and strategies, supported by pedagogical cases that show what Meaningful Physical Education can look like in school-based teaching and in higher education–based teacher education.

With an emphasis on good pedagogical practice, this is essential reading for all pre-service and in-service physical education teachers or coaches working in youth sport.

Tim Fletcher is Associate Professor in Physical Education at Brock University in Canada. His research interests are in teacher socialisation, teacher learning, and pedagogies for teaching Meaningful Physical Education, often using self-study of teacher education practice methodology to conduct his research. He co-hosts a website and blog focused on pedagogies of Meaningful Physical Education for practitioners.

Déirdre Ní Chróinín is a physical education teacher educator at the primary level in the Department of Arts Education and Physical Education, Mary Immaculate College in Ireland. Her current research is focused on the promotion of meaningful experiences for children and young people in sport and physical activity settings.

Douglas Gleddie is Professor in the Faculty of Education at the University of Alberta, Canada. He teaches physical education curriculum and pedagogy to undergraduate students. He also teaches graduate courses in health and physical education, reflective practice, physical literacy and research methods. His research foci include: narratives of physical education; school sport; physical literacy praxis; Meaningful Physical Education; and teacher education.

Stephanie Beni is a doctoral student studying physical education at Brock University in Canada. Her current research interests lie in identifying practical pedagogical strategies by which practitioners may promote a focus on meaningful experiences in physical education and physical activities contexts and in teachers' professional learning in physical education.

Routledge Focus on Sport Pedagogy
Series editor Ash Casey
Loughborough University, UK

The field of sport pedagogy (physical education and coaching) is united by the desire to improve the experiences of young people and adult participants. The *Routledge Focus on Sport Pedagogy* series presents small books on big topics in an effort to eradicate the boundaries that currently exist between young people, adult learners, coaches, teachers and academics, in schools, clubs and universities. Theoretically grounded but with a strong emphasis on practice, the series aims to open up important and useful new perspectives on teaching, coaching and learning in sport and physical education.

Perspectives on Game-Based Coaching
Edited by Shane Pill

The Game-Centred Approach to Sport Literacy
Sixto González-Víllora, Javier Fernandez-Rio, Eva Guijarro and Manuel Jacob Sierra-Díaz

Meaningful Physical Education
An Approach for Teaching and Learning
Edited by Tim Fletcher, Déirdre Ní Chróinín, Douglas Gleddie and Stephanie Beni

For more information about this series, please visit: www.routledge.com/
Routledge-Focus-on-Sport-Pedagogy/book-series/RFSPED

Meaningful Physical Education

An Approach for Teaching and Learning

Edited by Tim Fletcher, Déirdre Ní Chróinín, Douglas Gleddie and Stephanie Beni

Routledge
Taylor & Francis Group

LONDON AND NEW YORK

First published 2021
by Routledge
2 Park Square, Milton Park, Abingdon, Oxon OX14 4RN

and by Routledge
52 Vanderbilt Avenue, New York, NY 10017

Routledge is an imprint of the Taylor & Francis Group, an informa business

© 2021 selection and editorial matter Tim Fletcher, Déirdre
Ní Chróinín, Douglas Gleddie and Stephanie Beni; individual
chapters, the contributors

The right of Tim Fletcher, Déirdre Ní Chróinín, Douglas Gleddie
and Stephanie Beni to be identified as the authors of the editorial
material, and of the authors for their individual chapters, has been
asserted in accordance with sections 77 and 78 of the Copyright,
Designs and Patents Act 1988.

British Library Cataloguing-in-Publication Data
A catalogue record for this book is available from the British Library

Library of Congress Cataloging-in-Publication Data
Names: Fletcher, Tim (Educator) editor. | Ní Chróinín, Déirdre,
    editor. | Gleddie, Doug, 1971– | Beni, Stephanie, editor.
Title: Meaningful physical education : an approach for teaching
    and learning / Edited by Tim Fletcher, Déirdre Ní Chróinín,
    Douglas Gleddie, and Stephanie Beni.
Description: Abingdon, Oxon ; New York, NY : Routledge,
    2021. | Series: Routledge focus on sport pedagogy | Includes
    bibliographical references and index.
Identifiers: LCCN 2020053459 | ISBN 9780367473617 (hardback) |
    ISBN 9781003035091 (ebook)
Subjects: LCSH: Physical education and training—Study and
    teaching. | Physical education and training—Study and
    teaching (Higher) | Physical education and training—Study and
    teaching—Case studies.
Classification: LCC GV361 .M43 2021 | DDC 796.071—dc23
LC record available at https://lccn.loc.gov/2020053459

ISBN: 978-0-367-47361-7 (hbk)
ISBN: 978-1-032-00234-7 (pbk)
ISBN: 978-1-003-03509-1 (ebk)

Typeset in Times New Roman
by Apex CoVantage, LLC

TF: For Abby and Nathan, with hopes you find and thrive in your movement playgrounds

DNC: For Keara and Vince with love, thank you for helping to sculpt and scaffold my physical activity worlds

DG: For my students: past, present and future. May you find movement meaningful and create spaces for your physical education students to experience the same.

SB: For my students, with whom I have had the privilege of sharing the meaningfulness of movement. I hope you learn as much from me as I do from you.

Contents

Figures

Tables

Contributors

Michelle Alberts is Vice Principal in Physical Education and Sport Sciences teacher at Ecole Secondaire Highwood High School, Canada.

Alex Beckey is a participation specialist in PE at the Centre for PE, Sport and Activity at Kingston University, UK. Previously he was a secondary PE teacher, Head of PE and Director of Sport for 17 years, working both in the state and independent sectors.

Laura Boudens teaches Kindergarten to Grade 6 Health and Physical Education in Canada. Her career also includes teaching K-12 PE in China and Germany.

Richard Bowles works in the Department of Arts Education & Physical Education at Mary Immaculate College, Ireland, and teaches physical education in undergraduate and postgraduate primary/elementary teacher education programs. He also volunteers as a coach with some of the college's Gaelic football teams. Richard's research interests include school and community sport, teacher and coach education, and self-study research methodologies.

Maura Coulter is based in the Institute of Education at Dublin City University, Ireland, and teaches at both undergraduate and postgraduate levels. She has also coached a variety of sports to children aged 4–10 including swimming, rugby, gymnastics and camogie. Maura's research interests include Meaningful PE, teacher educator identity, pre-service teacher experiences and outdoor and adventure activities.

Nadeen Halls teaches Health and Physical Education (HPE) in Canada. Her career includes teaching students in Kindergarten through to Grade 12. Nadeen now serves as a past president of the Health and Physical Education Council (HPEC) of the Alberta Teacher's Association. Nadeen is a passionate advocate for Comprehensive School Health as a whole school approach to improving student well-being and achievement.

Jodi Harding-Kuriger is a health and physical educator for the joy and love of movement. She is dedicated to lifelong learning through the University of Alberta, Canada, and HPEC.

Autumn Nesdoly is a PhD student in the Faculty of Kinesiology, Sport, and Recreation at the University of Alberta, Canada. Her research interests are broadly focused on enhancing the sport and physical education experiences of youth. Outside of academia, Autumn is a competitive jump rope coach (and semi-retired athlete).

Mary O'Sullivan is recently retired from the University of Limerick, Ireland, where she served as Dean of the Faculty of Education and Health Sciences and Professor of Physical Education. Mary is currently Chair of the National Council for Curriculum and Assessment (NCCA) in Ireland. Mary's research interests have been on teaching, teachers and teacher education policy and practice, with a particular interest in Physical Education curriculum and pedagogy.

Ty Riddick is a health & physical education teacher at the Dr. Morris Gibson School in Canada.

Tony Sweeney is a lecturer with the Froebel Department of Primary and Early Childhood Education at Maynooth University, Ireland. His research includes Meaningful PE, Adapted Physical Education and the use of technology to support literacy.

Milena Trojanovic has been a physical educator in Ontario, Canada, for 28 years, teaching students from Kindergarten through Grade 8. She has had the opportunity to develop and present physical activity resources over the course of her career with her local school board as well as provincial organizations including CIRA Ontario and Ophea, and values ongoing personal professional development learning opportunities such as the MPE project.

Andy Vasily is a pedagogical coordinator, workshop leader, and podcaster based at the King Abdullah University of Science and Technology in Saudi Arabia. Andy has committed himself to better understanding how to design and deliver more meaningful learning experiences in physical education and is passionate about the work he does training physical educators around the world.

Foreword

.

I have always considered the many physical activities that have graced my life over the years more as adventures than duties. When I was a camp counselor, coach and skill instructor, I taught toward the adventure . . . or at least, I tried to do so. I always believed that duty-focused physical education was more a default position than a sound practice. Teachers who could not help students grow one or more personal movement playgrounds had to settle for something less – usually getting students' heart rates up and explaining why exercise is good for them.

Eleanor Metheny, one of my professors in graduate school, was not a friend of default-position physical education. She was driven to find answers to a single question, perhaps the single most important question a physical educator can ask: 'How does a movement mean?' It is a shame we have not asked it more often. It is a shame our pedagogies have not been built around answers to that question more regularly.

We know that answers are not easy to come by. Meaning is like a number of other elusive concepts. You know it when you see it, but it is hard to describe it in its absence. Fortunately, most of us have seen it. Meaningful movement has impacted our quality of life for the better. Our personal stories have been shaped by it. We identify ourselves as bikers, swimmers, table tennis players, hikers. We do not need to be told that delight can be found running across a grassy field or careening down snowy mountain slope.

The trick is to find ways to help others negotiate the same journey. How do you help another person grow a movement playground? The ideas and personal testimonies provided in the following pages of this wonderful volume help to answer that question.

The authors remind us the journey needs to respect individual differences – different cultural backgrounds, body types and ways of thinking. It needs to include 'just right' challenges and generate the deep satisfactions that accompany genuine achievements. It must be intrinsically enjoyable. It should honor the important role of motor competence in fostering this enjoyment. It goes better with the assistance of playmates, fellow travelers, friends. It should aim beyond enjoyment to those memorable experiences we identify as delightful.

It is a pleasure to see a volume on physical education pedagogy that focuses on the subjective, on affect and on that slippery thing called meaning. Since the urging of educators like John Dewey and since the onset of the progressive education movement well over a century ago, educators have voiced a commitment to teach the whole child. That commitment for physical educators will not be realized unless and until we return to Eleanor Metheny's question and take it seriously. Indeed, how *does* a movement mean?

R. Scott Kretchmar
Professor Emeritus
Department of Kinesiology
Penn State University
USA

Series editor introduction

In reading this book I was reminded of a hall of mirrors. Not the funny sort with concave and convex mirrors that make you look taller or shorter or wider or thinner, but the sort where multiple reflections surround you and you get to see 'things' from multiple angles. As such, this shouldn't be seen as a 'how to' book. This is not a step-by-step guide. Instead, it is a series of reflections on how different people in different contexts took up the challenge of enacting Meaningful PE. This is a book centred on pedagogy – on the irreducible relationship between curriculum, teaching, learning and assessment – and on the aspirations of Meaningful PE. There is no prescription in these pages but the acknowledgement that learning is an aspiration that comes through a transactional process of experience in unique and ever-changing environments.

This book reminds me much more of a conversation than a lecture. It is an introduction to an idea and the freedom to pursue the details in the spaces each practitioner knows best and with the students they value most. This reminds me very much of the aspirations David Kirk and I had for our newest book, and it resonates strongly with our vision of local agency and a subject built on specifications of practice rather than prescriptions. I suspect, though, that that is a conversation that needs to be had over dinner once we emerge from the throws of the global pandemic. Who's making the reservation?

Ash Casey
November 12, 2020

Reference

Casey, A., & Kirk, D. (2021). *Models-based practice in physical education*. London: Routledge.

Acknowledgements

We thank students enrolled in the graduate course on Meaningful Physical Education at the University of Alberta in the Winter of 2020. Your ideas and feedback have helped us clarify our ideas and thinking. We also thank the teachers, pre-service teachers and school students who have volunteered to participate in our research over the past several years and with whom we have engaged on social media, at conferences and in classrooms. The insights and perspectives you have provided have helped confirm some hunches but more importantly, have helped us develop more questions about how to help teachers prioritize meaningful experiences for students. Thanks also to Simon Whitmore at Routledge, the reviewers of our proposal, and to Ash Casey as the series editor for helping turn our ideas into a book – without your support we would not be able to share some of our stories and those of people with whom we have worked. Special thanks also go to R. Scott Kretchmar for writing the Foreword and for the many, many years of thinking and writing that have been so inspiring to us and that have led to concrete changes in our thinking and practices, and those of others. Yours are the shoulders upon which we stand.

This edited book draws on research funded by the Social Sciences and Humanities Research Council of Canada and by the Teaching Council of Ireland.

Abbreviations

LAMPE	Learning About Meaningful Physical Education
Meaningful PE	Meaningful Physical Education
PETE	Physical Education Teacher Education

Part I

Introducing Meaningful Physical Education

1 The why, what, and how of Meaningful Physical Education

*Tim Fletcher, Déirdre Ní Chróinín,
Douglas Gleddie and Stephanie Beni*

Introduction

We believe in the inherent value of movement in our lives and the lives of the students we teach. When meaningfulness is prioritized, students' experiences in physical education have the potential to enrich the quality of their lives (Kretchmar, 2008). Prioritizing the facilitation of meaningful experiences has the potential to shift the focus of current physical education programs to better meet the needs of contemporary learners (Quennerstedt, 2019).

Ideas about prioritizing meaningful physical education are not especially new; they are present in the physical education and sport pedagogy literature throughout the past 50 years, with scholars arguing for the inherent value potential of movement as a site of meaning-making to enhance human existence (Arnold, 1979; Chen, 1998; Ennis, 2017; Jewett & Bain, 1985; Kretchmar, 2007; Metheny, 1968; O'Connor, 2019). These arguments are also complemented by recent developments in the field of positive psychology where it is recognized that meaning and meaningfulness are valued concepts to clarify questions of human well-being and flourishing (Leontiev, 2013). By prioritizing meaningfulness in physical education, teachers would work with children and youth to identify features of an experience that are meaningful to them, such as those that are enjoyable, challenging, involve important opportunities for learning across several domains, and are personally relevant; the types of intrinsically motivating experiences that are likely to lead to a commitment to active participation (Teixeira, Carraça, Markland, Silva, & Ryan, 2012). Through collaboration with their teachers, children and youth may develop a deeper awareness of what they find meaningful and may be more likely to seek out these types of experiences in other contexts beyond physical education. There is, however, limited guidance for teachers in how they might promote meaningful experiences in physical education.

As part of the Routledge Focus on Sport Pedagogy series, we aim to provide clear descriptions of how several practitioners (teachers and teacher educators) have used the idea of meaningful experiences as the main filter for their pedagogical decisions and actions. Bringing together these descriptions has allowed us to develop a prototypical outline of the Meaningful Physical Education (Meaningful PE) approach, which we articulate in this chapter. The Meaningful PE approach offers guidance to support how practitioners can identify and enhance the quality of physical education experiences for learners. Fundamentally, we argue that greater attention to the meaningfulness of experience can promote richer and more impactful learning for young people in physical education to influence the quality of their ongoing engagement with movement and physical activity participation.

What do we mean by meaningful?

Kretchmar (2007) defines meaning 'in a broad, common sense way. It includes all emotions, perceptions, hopes, dreams, and other cognitions – in short, the full range of human experience' (p. 382). All experiences therefore have meaning in that the individual interprets and makes sense of the experience through attaching a value, symbol, or emotion to it. However, often the noun *meaning* has been conflated with the adjective *meaningful*. Meaningfulness is an individual and subjective construct that entails a value judgement(s) or interpretation of the meaning of circumstances (Baumeister, Vohs, Aaker, & Garbinsky, 2013).

Metheny (1968) suggests an experience becomes meaningful when 'we seize upon it, take it into ourselves, and become involved with it' (p. 5). Meaningfulness is therefore an interpretation of the significance something holds for an individual and involves the participant becoming aware and making sense of an experience in relation to past, present, and future experiences through a process of synthesis and reconciliation (Jarvis, 1987). Many psychologists now generally accept that meaningfulness involves a tripartite structure: a) *purpose*: a motivational component, related to goals, aims, and direction; b) *feelings of significance*: an emotional component involving evaluation of life's inherent value and worth; and c) *coherence*: a cognitive component related to understanding of one's life making sense and being comprehensible (Martela & Steger, 2016). Based on these proposals, it follows that meaningfulness in physical education involves considering the purposes and goals of movement, judgements related to the emotional value of the experience, and a sense of coherence where physical education can be connected to other life experiences (Chen, 1998). Based on this definition, the primary theme of Meaningful PE is to *support students in coming to value physical education through experiencing meaningfulness (i.e., interpreting an experience as having personal significance) and recognizing ways participation enhances the quality of their lives.*

Why Meaningful PE?

A consideration of why to use Meaningful PE begins with questioning one's overarching vision or philosophy for teaching. For us (and the other contributing authors), prioritizing meaningful experiences is crucial if we want children to experience some of the things in and about movement culture that have been and are so central to the quality of our own lives. It has become part of our individual and collective vision for physical education (Ní Chróinín, Beni, Fletcher, Griffin, & Price, 2019). We want children to walk through the doors of a gym or dance studio or enter onto a field, hiking trail, bike path, or body of water and be filled with a sense of excitement, joy, and adventure rather than dread, boredom, or fear. Beyond our personal beliefs and perspectives, however, there are some other broader reasons that support our position.

In many contexts there is a current emphasis on what we and some others see as a narrow set of utilitarian, health-based outcomes for young people where disease prevention through personal fitness is privileged over seeking the joy of movement. Along with others (Ennis, 2017; Kretchmar, 2008; Lambert, 2020; O'Connor, 2019; Thorburn, 2018), we resist this view, arguing that physical education is better positioned as an opportunity for students to engage in active participation in ways that make experiences more meaningful and enrich their lives. As Kretchmar (2006) suggests: 'one of the greatest things about physical activity and play is that they make our lives go better, not just longer. It is the quality of life, the joy of being alive' (p. 6). In this way, Meaningful physical education places the quality and personal significance of students' experiences at the forefront of a teacher's pedagogical decision-making (Kretchmar, 2008).

Prioritizing meaningful experiences also links to some of the major purposes of physical education, represented in policy documents and also in the beliefs and values of key stakeholders (such as teachers, students, parents, and administrators). Major analyses identify a range of benefits for young people that are linked to participation in physical education. For example, Engström (2008) identified several ways in which physical education supports learners' participation in active lifestyles well into adulthood. This may be reflected in learners achieving increased motor competence or learning to value and participate in a physically active lifestyle that reflects social and cultural awareness of individuals, communities, and the environment (McEvoy, Heikinaro-Johansson, & MacPhail, 2017). We take a slightly broader view of the overall purposes of physical education, aligning ourselves with the purpose of democratic transformation (Ennis, 2017), where 'different ways of being in the world as some-body are both possible and encouraged' (Quennerstedt, 2019, p. 611). In this way, education is viewed as a continual transforming of experience, with an aim of cultivating experiences that lead to the growth of further experience (Dewey, 1938). Although we aim to emphasize the positive qualities and values of a meaningful experience (those that encourage further exploration and participation), at times a meaningful experience might also have a negative value (e.g., unpleasant interpersonal interactions or finding a challenge 'beyond reach'). Dewey (1938) distinguishes these experiences by describing them as educative and mis-educative, with educative experiences being those whereby the individual seeks continuity of the experience rather than avoidance. Educative experiences that prompt reflection tend to produce powerful learning (Rodgers, 2002). From this perspective, having learners seek and become aware of the personal meaning of movement through reflection becomes part of the core purpose of physical education, where it is understood as a 'suitable learning context for initiation into a range of worthwhile social and cultural practices' (Thorburn, 2018, p. 26).

What is Meaningful PE based on and what does it consist of?

In finding an experience meaningful, attention is drawn to its quality, which influences the likelihood of individuals seeking the experience again or avoiding it. According to Dewey (1938, p. 44) individuals attach value to the experience 'because of a transaction taking place' between an individual and aspects of the environment, which in physical education could be: peers; the teacher; the gymnasium, swimming pool, dance studio, or playing field; objects such as balls, nets, or apparatus; or the tasks that represent subject matter (Quennerstedt, Almqvist, & Öhman, 2011). Personal meaning transactions and interpretations are therefore not constructed solely within but in relation to culture (Bruner, 1990), where individuals make connections to 'something that reaches beyond the actual experience, linking it to something else' (Leontiev, 2013, p. 462). Thus, attending closely to the meaningfulness of experiences necessitates consideration of the ways in which meaningfulness involves a complex mix of individual cognitive and affective elements as well as relational, social, and cultural dimensions. By aligning Meaningful PE with a transformative purpose and recognizing the social nature of learning, social constructivism serves as an appropriate theoretical basis upon which to ground its teaching and learning principles. Social constructivist perspectives 'focus on the interdependence of social and individual processes in the co-construction of knowledge' (Palincsar, 1998, p. 345).

Pedagogically, our approach is built from a major review of literature we conducted on studies focused on meaningful experiences in physical education and youth sport since 1987. We drew from Kretchmar's (2006) assertion that meaningful experiences in physical education tend to consist of several features: social interaction, challenge, fun, motor competence, and delight. In that review of 50 peer-reviewed empirical research studies, we found support for the first four of those features, while adding another: personally relevant learning (Beni, Fletcher, & Ní Chróinín, 2017). Although we did not find empirical support for delight, we believe it is worthy to acknowledge because it supports a perspective that physical education can promote 'temporary and special affective states that are memorable in their own right but are also motivators for additional delights at higher levels of skill, knowledge and understanding' (Kretchmar, 2005, p. 205).

Social interaction: Teachers should carefully consider how opportunities for social interaction are organized and structured based on students' needs and desires. Social interaction can occur in positive ways, supporting ongoing participation (Light, 2010), learning (Lyngstad, Bjerke, & Lagestad, 2020), and a sense of accomplishment, particularly when working in teams (Domville, Watson, Richardson, & Graves, 2019; Koekoek & Knoppers, 2015; Ní Chróinín, Fletcher, & Griffin, 2018). This requires consideration of all relationships in the learning environment (e.g., student-student, student-teacher) and therefore, teachers should aim to foster a strongly developed sense of community in the classroom (Azzarito & Ennis, 2003).

Challenge: Kretchmar (2006) identifies 'just-right' or optimal challenges as essential to enticing children to enter and invest in developing their personal playgrounds. Optimal challenges possess the lure of success, which can be achieved with sufficient support, time, effort, persistence, and patience (Mandigo & Holt, 2006). Dyson (1995) showed that when students were provided with opportunities to choose their level of challenge, they found physical education more meaningful. Challenge can also serve as motivation to continued participation. Students in a study by Gillison, Sebire, and Standage (2012) felt motivated by appropriate levels of challenge because they were provided with: a sense of achievement, explicit outcomes which served as reasons to try an activity, the option to set one's own goals, and self-improvement in skills or fitness. Inappropriate levels of challenge can have harmful effects on participation – when the level of challenge is too easy or too hard, it can induce boredom, which leads to apathy (i.e., 'meaninglessness') toward physical education (Dismore & Bailey, 2011). Careful consideration should be given to the presentation of competition, as some children thrive in interpersonal competition while others do not. A balanced approach to competition might involve avoiding activities that emphasize winning more than learning, the use of alternative scoring systems that reward aspects of participation beyond winning (e.g., spirit points to reward positive social behaviours), and encouraging a focus on achieving personal bests. This can be done by having students set personal process-oriented goals across domains during competitive activities, such as encouraging teammates, limiting erroneous decisions in game play, or focusing on efficient or consistent skill execution.

Fun: Fun has been identified by students in primary/elementary (Dyson, 1995) and high school (Dismore & Bailey, 2011) as contributing to the meaningfulness they experience in physical education. However, the reasons for physical education being fun differ across the age/grade levels: primary students often identify playing games, running around (or similar), and being with friends as sources of fun, while secondary students sometimes interpret fun in relation to challenge and learning (Dismore & Bailey, 2011). There is debate about the place of fun in physical education (e.g., Quennerstedt, 2013), however, many children identify fun as the main reason they continue to participate; its absence can be a deal breaker when children evaluate their experiences (Ladwig, Vazou, & Ekkekakis, 2018). While fun alone is too low an aim, it can result in new or existing relationships, motivation, increased effort, and learning (Hopple, 2018; Kretchmar, 2006). We position fun as a vehicle for learning and engagement, a necessary but often insufficient condition for experiences to be ascribed as meaningful. Fun should be considered in the context of learning, where the absence of learning is as problematic for teachers as the absence of fun is for students.

Motor competence: Physical education is more positive when students perceive they are competent in performing skills associated with tasks, while lack of competence can inhibit enjoyment and social interaction and detract from meaningfulness. Secondary students often put more effort into physical education when their perceived competence is high (Gray, Sproule, & Wang 2008). While motor competence is a central feature of Meaningful PE, we caution against an overemphasis on skill performance over other types of learning. Beni, Fletcher, and Ní Chróinín (2019) showed that children valued motor competence but also recognized the contributions that social and cognitive competence made to a meaningful experience. Moreover, overemphasizing skill performance above all else can also exclude or isolate some students (Fitzgerald, 2005).

Personally relevant learning: Helping children make connections between physical education and other pursuits outside of school is important in promoting children's ongoing commitment to an active lifestyle; however, many children lack an understanding of how physical education relates to out-of-school activities (Parker, MacPhail, O'Sullivan, Chróinín, & McEvoy, 2018). Children need to understand *what* they are learning, *why* this learning can be important, and *how* this learning can be applied to their lives. Teachers should therefore actively make connections and explain reasons why things are being learned, but also offer content that is accessible and culturally/contextually relevant to students (Braga, Elliott, Jones, & Bulger, 2015).

Delight: According to Kretchmar (2005, p. 202), delight 'first and foremost, is a memorable experience. Its subjective qualities are such that it stands out from the ordinary'. Elsewhere, Kretchmar (2006) distinguishes delight from other concepts, stating: 'Delight is different from fun, just as "love" is different from "like", and "excellence" is not the same thing as "competence"' (p. 7). Delight is more enduring than fun and grounded in 'powerful intrinsic satisfactions' (Kretchmar, 2008, p. 162). Delight attaches itself to genuine achievements and is a 'condition of rest, of fulfilment . . . to experience delight, one must achieve a close tie with something that is desirable but often lies at a distance or is typically out of reach' (Kretchmar, 2005, p. 205). Young people did not identify delight as contributing to a meaningful physical education experience (Beni et al., 2017), perhaps because it is such an elusive concept and is therefore challenging to articulate. Moreover, delight is not easily planned for, and as such, a teacher might aim to provide meaningful experiences in physical education such that students may experience delight in their own time through engagement with their own personal playgrounds.

While children in many of the articles reviewed often referred to one or more of these features as major contributors to how they experienced meaningful experiences in physical education (e.g., 'I found it meaningful because I was challenged'), the features usually worked together and were therefore more integrated than isolated (e.g., 'Today was fun because I got to be in a group with my friends and we spoke about playing the same game at the park this weekend'). Modifications to a task based on one of the features can therefore have an impact on the others (e.g., adjusting the level of challenge can have effects on fun and students' engagement with motor competence). It would not be expected that all features necessarily be present in all lessons or that each feature be given equal weight (see Chapter 5). Rather, decisions will need to be made based on the outcomes selected for student learning in conjunction with their needs and interests within each unique context and the teacher's own beliefs.

Elsewhere we have shown how the features can be used to guide teachers' and teacher educators' decisions as they occur lesson-to-lesson (guiding overall lesson and unit planning) and in the moment (Fletcher, Ní Chróinín, & O'Sullivan, 2019). We are open to the possibility that in a given context some of these principles and features may be unsuitable or inappropriate for a variety of reasons. It is therefore important that teachers draw on their own expertise and judgement to make decisions. We are also very mindful that these features likely do not paint a complete picture of what might contribute to learners finding a physical education experience meaningful. For instance, we think that creativity and self-expression are but some of the other things that could contribute to how some students experience meaningfulness and suggest to teachers that the features identified by Beni et al. (2017) are not used in a reductive sense but as a useful basis upon which to begin conversing with students about what they find meaningful in physical education.

How do I teach using Meaningful PE?

In response to some early experimentation with ideas about Meaningful PE, we and others have relied largely on using the features of Meaningful PE (both those described earlier and those identified by students independently) to facilitate a shared language in the physical education class. These ideas have been helpful to address some gaps in the knowledge of how to prioritize meaningfulness and think about what Meaningful PE is and how we might support children to enter into and become immersed in movement cultures (Kretchmar, 2000). At the same time, we feel there is more to it than asking students whether they had fun, were challenged, and so on. That is, there are both broad and specific principles and strategies that work well in supporting students in, for example, interacting positively with others, experiencing optimal levels of challenge, developing motor competence, having fun, and seeing the personal relevance in what they are learning in physical education. Alongside these features, analysis of the nature of meaningfulness outlined previously provides direction on what pedagogies of meaningfulness entail. In particular, the retrospective and personal characteristics of meaningfulness point to the value of reflective and democratic pedagogies as central to Meaningful PE. In the following sections we identify key strategies that facilitate meaningfulness in ways that reflect the spirit of Meaningful PE as both *democratic* and *reflective*.

We offer Meaningful PE as a provisional and flexible set of ideas that can help teachers *and students* make decisions about how to facilitate meaningful experiences in physical education. Meaningful PE can be applied across all physical education content (e.g., dance, gymnastics, aquatics, games) and linked to the particular outcomes and expectations of official curriculum and policy documents across various contexts. While we see Meaningful PE as having characteristics that make it distinct from other approaches (that is, the prioritization of facilitating meaningful experiences for students), we also aim to position it in such a way that it may bring together seemingly disparate or competing ideas and models in physical education, thus reducing fragmentation and improving coherence in the field (O'Connor & Jess, 2020). It is therefore not offered 'in competition' with other models and approaches to teaching physical education. Rather, we see Meaningful PE as an overarching framework, informing how models and approaches are selected and implemented.

Meaningful PE is democratic

Democratic principles (Thorburn, 2018) lie at the heart of the Meaningful PE approach. Meaningful experiences require personal investment, ownership of learning, and personal relevance in ways that demand a democratic approach. In this way, Meaningful PE is, at its core, *inclusive* and promotes 'genuinely pluralistic physical education practices' and outcomes (Quennerstedt, 2019, p. 611) by supporting a variety of learning needs and interests. This involves teachers and students working together to set goals and agree on activities within a flexible curriculum 'as close to the learners as possible' (Ennis, 2017). In this way, the teacher and students are positioned as learning collaborators, as students want increased opportunities for *autonomy* and agency so that they are able to make choices about their experiences and to use their voices to contribute to the planning and delivery of physical education (Enright & O'Sullivan, 2010). Autonomy-supportive strategies promote intrinsic forms of motivation, which have been shown to facilitate longer commitment to active participation across the lifespan (Teixeira et al., 2012).

Teachers should aim to be student-centred in much of their decision-making, providing students with more control of their experience to engage with tasks that have personal relevance and carry out activities they find meaningful in their own right. For example, teachers can involve students in planning decisions by actively seeking input on unit design and being responsive to students' perspectives. The involvement of children in genuine dialogue within democratic processes can help them learn to mediate personal and cultural elements, to negotiate with each other and with teachers to compromise in making and enacting collective decisions (Dyson, 1995). This is not to imply 'anything goes' or that children's preferences can always be accommodated, but rather, through discussion and negotiation students can be supported in engaging with and finding some value in physical activity experiences that may not be appealing initially or be given alternatives to draw them into an experience. Students might collaborate with teachers to make decisions about the type, nature, and duration of tasks (Enright & O'Sullivan, 2010). They might also make decisions about how they participate in tasks, such as selecting roles to take on in a Sport Education unit based on their personal interest. A degree of developmental appropriateness should be considered when making decisions about how much choice to give students and how to involve them in decision-making; it is recommended that both be gradually introduced to ensure children are not overwhelmed, as this opportunity and responsibility may be unfamiliar to them (Beni et al., 2019). It is expected that the level of co-construction would increase developmentally with age.

This also requires the teacher to be intentional about how they promote both student-student and student-teacher relationships. Teaching qualities that promote positive interaction include counselling, listening, questioning, honesty, playfulness, a sense of humour, and self-reflection. General strategies to help students feel they matter are using students' names when giving encouragement, smiling and making eye contact, showing interest in and respect for each student, and sharing attention evenly around the class. Models such as Sport Education, Teaching for Personal and Social Responsibility, or Cooperative Learning offer opportunities and learning experiences that support positive social interaction.

In addition to offering opportunities to make choices and be involved in decision-making, other characteristics of autonomy-supportive classrooms include listening to children and providing time for independent work, acknowledging others' perspectives and feelings, and praising improvement and effort (Mandigo & Holt, 2006). Strategies that support students in making autonomous decisions about their engagement include: selecting specific tasks based on personal level of interest or challenge; contributing to group composition decisions (Koekoek & Knoppers, 2015); modifying tasks to tailor the level of challenge to individual skill levels; and identifying tasks to be assessed in culminating activities (Beni et al., 2019). The use of parallel activities during lessons, for example, where one is competitive and one is not, or one is team-based and one is a paired/individual activity, provides opportunities for students to make choices about their participation and inform how they might make similar choices in the future and identify preferred forms of engagement.

In facilitating these types of experiences the teacher thus serves as an 'activity broker' (Kretchmar, 2000) who is motivated to plan meaningful experiences for and with students. Insight on students' needs and interests is therefore central to guiding pedagogical decision-making both prior to a lesson and in the moment. Being an activity broker requires an emphasis on student choice and responsibility, as well as a knowledge of the local communities where students can access physical activities that they find personally relevant, while also being aware of the barriers and facilitators to participation (for example, socioeconomic conditions). To help children make these connections, teachers can use community physical activity notice boards to promote local opportunities, plan field trips to local play venues, or invite guest speakers who might act as role models and contacts in helping children access opportunities outside of school. For example, teacher and blogger Andy Vasily offered a 'Connections to Community' unit, where his Grade 5 class visited local bike paths, skate parks, and playing fields (Vasily, 2018). Students were then encouraged to engage with their preferred activity and space with family and friends.

Meaningful PE is reflective

You will recall that meaningfulness in physical education is related to both the desire to achieve a purpose or goal of movement aligned with judgements related to the emotional value of the experience in striving to achieve the goal (Chen, 1998). Opportunities to set goals and to reflect on their achievement is central to identification of experiences as meaningful. Reflection in and on experience is therefore crucial in order for both teachers and students to identify and become aware of the meaning made from certain situations (Dewey, 1916). For teachers, both reflection in- and on-action can be used to consider the ways students are finding experiences meaningful. Teachers can gauge the quality of student experience in the lesson through observation and questioning; for example, a 'check-in' might involve the teacher asking students about the quality of experience of a particular task or whether the task is something they would like to pursue outside of school.

Reflective processes are also important for students to engage in so they may become aware of the ways they experience meaningfulness in physical education. Reflection is central in other examples of meaning-making pedagogies. For example, Standal (2015) suggests reflection is in itself a meaning-making process, moving 'the learner from one experience to the next' (p. 110) and helping develop a deeper understanding of the experience. Similarly, O'Connor (2019) involved students in guided reflection (narrative and silent) about the value of particular movement experiences. Beyond their personal experience in a task or activity, attention can also be drawn to discussions about physical activity participation in the wider community, through asking: Who has access? Who benefits? and Who is disadvantaged?

These discussions can help individuals make sense of their own experiences as well as promote actions towards a more socially just world.

In order to engage students in reflective processes, a teacher might use goal-setting, introduce a PE Diary, or use paired, small, and large group discussions during and after participation. *Goal-setting* can facilitate personally relevant learning for students where opportunities to transfer learning to their lives outside of school can be identified. We recommend identifying short- and long-term goals for student learning.

Using a poster to represent the features (both existing and those identified by students beyond what was supported in Beni et al., 2017) in developmentally appropriate language is one way to support students in understanding and making sense of things that they find meaningful on a recurring basis. Alternatives for difficult terms for young learners might include:

- Being with others (social interaction)
- Developing or getting better at skills (motor competence)
- Making connections (personally relevant learning)

Children can become increasingly familiar with the ideas of Meaningful PE if teachers consistently use a ***shared language*** to communicate learning outcomes and encourage students to set goals and reflect on their experiences. A reflective diary provides a space for students to identify the nature and extent of the meaning they make in physical education and make sense of their experiences (Ní Chróinín, Fletcher, & Griffin, 2018), while also serving as an assessment tool for teachers. Based on the centrality of reflection in order to understand and identify ways students make meaning and experience meaningfulness, we feel it is worth sacrificing some time for physical activity in a physical education lesson in order to embed reflective processes.

It is worth pointing out how our ideas about Meaningful PE as an approach for teachers is both similar and different to another approach we have written about: Learning About Meaningful Physical Education (LAMPE). LAMPE was developed as a framework to help teacher educators (i.e., those who teach teachers) support pre-service teachers in learning how to promote and prioritize meaningful experiences for the students with whom they will eventually work. Following several years of studying our own practices as teacher educators, we developed several pedagogical principles of LAMPE (Ní Chróinín, Fletcher, & O'Sullivan, 2018). These are referred to in more detail in Chapter 6. LAMPE differs slightly from Meaningful PE due to the learners involved. In LAMPE, pre-service teachers are positioned as learners while in Meaningful PE, school-aged students are learners. It is our hope that through LAMPE pre-service teachers may enact Meaningful PE as an approach in their teaching once they graduate and enter the workforce.

What lies ahead?

In this book we have gathered an international group of practitioners who describe their engagement with ideas related to Meaningful PE. Each has used some aspect of the Meaningful PE approach or LAMPE to enable them to prioritize meaningfulness for the learners with whom they work. You will notice that some authors use many parts of the approach (e.g., reference to the features of Meaningful PE, goal-setting, reflection, autonomy-supportive strategies, allowing students to make decisions), while others use a few parts. To us, this represents the flexibility of the approach. Because the Meaningful PE framework is relatively new, we aim to learn from these and other practitioners about the aspects of the approach that make sense and are effective based on the contexts in which they work, including the students' needs and interests, and the teacher's beliefs and values.

This is a practical book oriented towards guiding the application of Meaningful PE by practitioners. We have used bold, italicized text to highlight where and how the authors have used specific aspects of Meaningful PE (e.g., reflection, autonomy-support, use of the features) in each chapter. The book consists of four parts. The current chapter introduces the Meaningful PE approach and then the remainder of the book. Chapters in Parts II and III are written by practitioners in schools and universities, respectively. Each of these chapters follows a rough outline, including:

- the social contexts in which they are implementing Meaningful PE (who and where they are teaching) and why Meaningful PE is appropriate for their practice (particularly in terms of how the idea of meaningful experiences serves as a vision or philosophy of their respective practices and objective for students)
- what Meaningful PE consists of in their practice (in particular, how principles related to democratic and reflective practices, and the features of Meaningful PE are used)
- how they implemented some or all of the Meaningful PE approach in terms of pedagogical strategies and decision-making

The four chapters in Part II are written from the perspective of teachers, each of whom describes how they used the Meaningful PE approach with learners in K-12 schools. Part III consists of three chapters from teacher educators who have used ideas from the LAMPE project (Ní Chróinín, Fletcher, & O'Sullivan, 2018) to teach pre-service teachers in universities.

In Part IV, we provide a brief synopsis of Meaningful PE, offering several steps we feel might be helpful to teachers who want to implement Meaningful PE in their practice. Also in Part IV, several students (most of whom are also teachers) from a master's course on Meaningful Physical Education at the University of Alberta provide brief pedagogical cases based on their personal teaching experiences and interactions with Meaningful PE. Mary O'Sullivan also offers her thoughts about the chapters in the book and the future for Meaningful PE.

Fundamentally, in this book we argue for greater attention to be given to the meaningfulness of PE experiences, in order to promote richer and more impactful learning that influences the quality of participants' engagement with physical activity participation, now and in the future. We hope that practitioners who work in a variety of contexts and with a variety of learners find some of the ideas useful in supporting their practice(s), and ultimately, to make physical education meaningful to the people for whom physical education is designed: our students.

References

Arnold, P. J. (1979). *Meaning in movement, sport and physical education.* London: Heinemann.

Azzarito, L., & Ennis, C. D. (2003). A sense of connection: Toward social constructivist physical education. *Sport, Education and Society, 8,* 179–198.

Baumeister, R. F., Vohs, K. D., Aaker, J. L., & Garbinsky, E. N. (2013). Some key differences between a happy life and a meaningful life. *The Journal of Positive Psychology, 8,* 505–516.

Beni, S., Fletcher, T., & Ní Chróinín, D. (2017). Meaningful experiences in physical education and youth sport: A review of the literature. *Quest, 69,* 291–312.

Beni, S., Fletcher, T., & Ní Chróinín, D. (2019). Using features of meaningful experiences to guide primary physical education practice. *European Physical Education Review, 25,* 599–615.

Braga, L., Elliott, E., Jones, E., & Bulger, S. (2015). Middle school students' perceptions of culturally and geographically relevant content in physical education. *International Journal of Kinesiology and Sports Science, 3,* 62–73.

Bruner, J. S. (1990). *Acts of meaning.* Cambridge, MA: Harvard University Press.

Chen, A. (1998). Meaningfulness in physical education: A description of high school students' conceptions. *Journal of Teaching in Physical Education, 17,* 285–306.

Dewey, J. (1916). *Democracy and education.* New York, NY: Palgrave Macmillan.

Dewey, J. (1938). *Experience and education.* New York, NY: Touchstone.

Dismore, H., & Bailey, R. (2011). Fun and enjoyment in physical education: Young people's attitudes. *Research Papers in Education, 26,* 499–516.

Domville, M., Watson, P. M., Richardson, D., & Graves, L. E. F. (2019). Children's perceptions of factors that influence PE enjoyment: A qualitative investigation. *Physical Education and Sport Pedagogy, 24,* 207–219.

Dyson, B. P. (1995). Students' voices in two alternative elementary physical education programs. *Journal of Teaching in Physical Education, 14*, 394–407.

Engström, L. M. (2008). Who is physically active? Cultural capital and sports participation from adolescence to middle age – a 38-year follow-up study. *Physical Education and Sport Pedagogy, 13*, 319–343.

Ennis, C. D. (2017). Educating students for a lifetime of physical activity: Enhancing mindfulness, motivation, and meaning. *Research Quarterly for Exercise and Sport, 88*, 241–250.

Enright, E., & O'Sullivan, M. (2010). 'Can I do it in my pyjamas?' Negotiating a physical education curriculum with teenage girls. *European Physical Education Review, 16*, 203–222.

Fitzgerald, H. (2005). Still feeling like a spare piece of luggage? Embodied experiences of (dis)ability in physical education and school sport. *Physical Education and Sport Pedagogy, 10*, 41–59.

Fletcher, T., Ní Chróinín, D., & O'Sullivan, M. (2019). Developing deep understanding of teacher education through accessing and responding to pre-service teacher engagement with their learning. *Professional Development in Education, 45*, 832–847.

Gillison, F., Sebire, S., & Standage, M. (2012). What motivates girls to take up exercise during adolescence? Learning from those who succeed. *British Journal of Health Psychology, 17*, 536–550.

Gray, S., Sproule, J., & Wang, C. K. J. (2008). Pupils' perceptions of and experiences in team invasion games: A case study of a Scottish secondary school and its three feeder primary schools. *European Physical Education Review, 14*, 179–201.

Hopple, C. J. (2018). Top 10 reasons why children find physical activity to be fun. *Strategies, 31*(3), 40–47.

Jarvis, P. (1987). Meaningful and meaningless experience: Towards an analysis of learning from life. *Adult Education Quarterly, 37*, 164–172.

Jewett, A., & Bain, L. L. (1985). *The curriculum process in physical education.* Dubuque, IA: Wm. C. Brown Publishers.

Koekoek, J., & Knoppers, A. (2015). The role of perceptions of friendships and peers in learning skills in physical education. *Physical Education and Sport Pedagogy, 20*, 231–249.

Kretchmar, R. S. (2000). Movement subcultures: Sites for meaning. *Journal of Physical Education, Recreation and Dance, 71*(5), 19–25.

Kretchmar, R. S. (2005). Teaching games for understanding and the delights of human activity. In L. L. Griffin & J. I. Butler (Eds.), *Teaching games for understanding, theory, research and practice* (pp. 119–212). Champaign, IL: Human Kinetics.

Kretchmar, R. S. (2006). Ten more reasons for quality physical education. *Journal of Physical Education, Recreation and Dance, 77*(9), 6–9.

Kretchmar, R. S. (2007). What to do with meaning? A research conundrum for the 21st century. *Quest, 59*, 373–383.

Kretchmar, R. S. (2008). The increasing utility of elementary school physical education: A mixed blessing and unique challenge. *The Elementary School Journal, 108*(3), 161–170.

Ladwig, M. A., Vazou, S., & Ekkekakis, P. (2018). 'My best memory Is when I was done with it': PE memories are associated with adult sedentary behavior. *Translational Journal of the American College of Sports Medicine, 3*(16), 119–129.

Lambert, K. (2020). Re-conceptualizing embodied pedagogies in physical education by creating pre-text vignettes to trigger pleasure 'in' movement. *Physical Education and Sport Pedagogy, 25,* 154–173.

Leontiev, D. A. (2013). Positive psychology in search for meaning: An introduction. *The Journal of Positive Psychology, 8,* 457–458.

Light, R. (2010). A cross-cultural study on meaning and the nature of children's experiences in Australian and French swimming clubs. *Asia-Pacific Journal of Health, Sport and Physical Education, 1*(3–4), 37–43.

Lyngstad, I., Bjerke, Ø., & Lagestad, P. (2020). Students' views on the purpose of physical education in upper secondary school. Physical education as a break in everyday school life – learning or just fun? *Sport, Education and Society, 25,* 230–241.

Mandigo, J. L., & Holt, N. L. (2006). Elementary students' accounts of optimal challenge in physical education. *Physical Educator, 63,* 170–183.

Martela, F., & Steger, M. F. (2016). The three meanings of meaning in life: Distinguishing coherence, purpose, and significance. *The Journal of Positive Psychology, 11,* 531–545.

McEvoy, E., Heikinaro-Johansson, P., & MacPhail, A. (2017). Physical education teacher educators' views regarding the purpose(s) of school physical education. *Sport, Education and Society, 22,* 812–824.

Metheny, E. (1968). *Movement and meaning.* New York, NY: McGraw-Hill.

Ní Chróinín, D., Beni, S., Fletcher, T., Griffin, C., & Price, C. (2019). Using meaningful experiences as a vision for physical education teaching and teacher education practice. *Physical Education and Sport Pedagogy, 24,* 598–614.

Ní Chróinín, D., Fletcher, T., & Griffin, C. (2018). Exploring pedagogies to promote meaningful participation in primary PE. *Physical Education Matters, 13*(2), 70–73.

Ní Chróinín, D., Fletcher, T., & O'Sullivan, M. (2018). Pedagogical principles of learning to teach meaningful physical education. *Physical Education and Sport Pedagogy, 23,* 117–133.

O'Connor, J. P. (2019). Exploring a pedagogy for meaning-making in physical education. *European Physical Education Review, 25,* 1093–1109.

O'Connor, J. P., & Jess, M. (2020). From silos to crossing borders in physical education. *Sport, Education and Society, 25,* 409–422.

Palincsar, A. S. (1998). Social constructivist perspectives on teaching and learning. *Annual Review of Psychology, 49,* 345–375.

Parker, M., MacPhail, A., O'Sullivan, M., Chróinín, D. N., & McEvoy, E. (2018). 'Drawing' conclusions: Irish primary school children's understanding of physical education and physical activity opportunities outside of school. *European Physical Education Review, 24,* 449–466.

Quennerstedt, M. (2013). PE on YouTube – investigating participation in physical education practice. *Physical Education and Sport Pedagogy, 18,* 42–59.

Quennerstedt, M. (2019). Physical education and the art of teaching: Transformative learning and teaching in physical education and sports pedagogy. *Sport, Education and Society, 24*, 611–623.

Quennerstedt, M., Almqvist, J., & Öhman, M. (2011). Keep your eye on the ball: Investigating artifacts-in-use in physical education. *Interchange, 42*, 287–305.

Rodgers, C. R. (2002). Seeing student learning: Teacher change and the role of reflection. *Harvard Educational Review, 72*, 230–253.

Standal, Ø. F. (2015). *Phenomenology and pedagogy in physical education.* Abingdon, UK: Routledge.

Teixeira, P. J., Carraça, E. V., Markland, D., Silva, M. N., & Ryan, R. M. (2012). Exercise, physical activity, and self-determination theory: A systematic review. *International Journal of Behavioral Nutrition and Physical Activity, 9*, 78–107.

Thorburn, M. (2018). John Dewey, subject purposes and schools of tomorrow: A centennial reappraisal of the educational contribution of physical education. *Learning, Culture and Social Interaction, 19*, 22–28.

Vasily, A. (2018, January 23). *Celebrating success: Empowerment and action through physical activity.* Retrieved October 1, 2018, from www.pyppewithandy.com/pyp-pe-blog/celebrating-success

Part II

Meaningful Physical Education by teachers

2 Meaningful Physical Education in an individual pursuits unit

Andy Vasily

Introduction

Physical activity, sport, and movement have always played a huge role in my life. The early experiences I had with physical activity and sport profoundly shaped my identity and provided me with a genuine sense of meaning and purpose in my life. These are some of the biggest reasons why the Meaningful PE approach has resonated so strongly with me as a teacher. It has also led me to work hard to better understand the approach and to think about how I can apply it to teaching and learning in physical education and beyond.

My purpose in this chapter is to describe how I have unpacked the Meaningful PE approach. I consider how the approach has influenced my planning decisions and explain the ways I have prioritized the feature of *challenge* with students in relation to their own PE experiences.

I believe that all of the *features* that contribute to meaningful experiences (i.e., challenge, social interaction, fun, motor competence, personal relevance, and delight) should be factored into a student's PE experiences. Each can play a significant role in helping students create strong and relevant connections in their lives, both inside and outside of school. However, in my own context, I was really drawn to learn more about how the feature of challenge could not only be prioritized but also unpacked with my students at a deeper level. This does not mean that the other features do not play an important part; quite the contrary, as they all seem to fall nicely into place as contributing to experiences of challenge.

I have designed this chapter to give a broad overview of why I felt it was important to prioritize the feature of challenge. I describe the context of my program and share the pedagogical decisions and actions I have made to unpack challenge in a way that hopefully allows all students to find their own entry points into learning in PE. Finally, I also describe the role that peer and self-assessment plays in helping students better understand the feature of challenge as it applies to their own learning and that of others in PE.

Before getting further, I want to help paint a better picture of who I am and my background. I am from Windsor, Ontario, and graduated with degrees in psychology and education before deciding to take the risk to go and experience the world beyond Canada. In 1997, my wife and I packed our bags, jumped on a plane, and began our journey teaching in Hiroshima, Japan, at one of their first International Baccalaureate (IB) schools. After quite a long stint teaching at this school, we realized how many opportunities there were to teach internationally. Being adventurous in spirit and having a passion for travel, we decided to explore what was possible.

We loved the IB approach to education and wanted to stay in the field. An IB education aims to develop inquiring, knowledgeable, and caring young people who help to create a better and more peaceful world through intercultural understanding and respect. With that in mind, much of my teaching over the years has heavily focused on inquiry and agency in order to provide each student with differentiated learning experiences as it relates to their skill development in PE. Keeping the IB spirit in mind with my own personal philosophy, we eventually moved on to teach at IB schools in Azerbaijan, Cambodia, and China. We presently work at The King Abdullah University of Science and Technology (KAUST) School in Saudi Arabia. Teaching internationally has been a richly rewarding experience that has opened our eyes to just how beautiful the world is, and we feel incredibly lucky to have met wonderful people from so many different cultures.

As I am on the leadership team at my present school and work as a pedagogical coach to support teachers' practice in different subjects, many of my responsibilities take me away from day-to-day teaching. However, I still try to co-teach PE (and other subjects) as much as possible. I never want to remove myself from teaching as I thoroughly enjoy spending time with students and learning how to better develop my teaching practice. This also gives me a better sense of how I can support other teachers with their practices.

As one can imagine, I have taught young people from all over the world. Although I have taught many different types of students from numerous backgrounds and cultures, the common thread that I have come to understand about young people is that their needs and abilities in relation to physical activity and sport vary greatly. Bearing that in mind, I have a strong belief that the only way I can provide a quality PE experience that addresses students' needs is to ultimately meet them at their own level of skill and ability.

Why did I choose to explore the Meaningful PE approach?

When I reflect on the powerful role that physical activity and sport have played in my own life, I see strong connections to the features of Meaningful PE. All my physical activity and sport experiences were genuinely joyful (***delight, fun***) and sparked within me a desire to ***challenge*** myself to build my own skills in order to strive for excellence in my pursuits. My ***motor competence*** took care of itself as I was always intrinsically motivated and driven to improve, so I practiced constantly. I also surrounded myself with others who had the same pursuits and interests as me (***social interaction***). Being connected with others through physical activity and sport made a big difference to me. Through these wonderful experiences, I was not only mentored by important people in my life, but also had opportunities to mentor others.

My learning and development as an athlete and lifelong mover were always ***personally relevant*** to me as I had autonomy and control over the choices I made about being active and learning how to improve the skills of my craft.

Through my many discussions with members of the PE community I became aware of the Meaningful PE approach. I worked closely with Tim Fletcher, who helped me develop a deeper understanding of the approach, which sparked my curiosity about how I could apply it in my own teaching context. As I reflected back on my own experiences with physical activity and sport, I was able to make strong connections to many features of Meaningful PE. This helped me to reframe what was possible regarding teaching and learning in PE.

What did I have to let go of to better embrace the Meaningful PE approach?

As my understanding of the Meaningful PE approach deepened, I was beginning to question some of the teaching beliefs I previously held close to my heart. For years I strongly believed that all students needed to learn a wide range of physical skills and to do so in quite a linear way. I thought this would help them better participate in physical activity and sport and be more engaged in PE. For example, if they could learn A, they would be able to do B, and by being able to do B, this would for sure transfer over to being able to do C.

Although these thoughts and actions came with good intentions, I came to realize that my time with students was limited. Despite always being an inquiry-based teacher, I needed to consider new ways of offering PE. This is when I began to explore the idea of differentiation in greater depth and the role it played in better addressing the needs of my students by genuinely meeting them at the point of their individual physical literacy journeys. I knew I needed to let go of some of my previous ways of teaching as they were too teacher-directed.

Some questions that came to mind as I reflected on my PE program were:

- Did I really have time to explicitly teach all the skills I wanted students to learn in PE?
- What were my students' roles as active participants in their own learning in PE?

- How might I better inspire students to find joy and a love of physical activity and sport under their own terms and conditions?
- How could I maximize opportunities for students to have much more voice and choice in their learning journeys?
- What connections existed between the feature of challenge and differentiated learning in PE?

Through responding to these questions, I began to see ways that I could not only use the feature of challenge to better plan my teaching in PE but to also be very explicit in the way that I unpacked that feature with my students. This process required me to actively involve students in unpacking what challenge meant to them as soon as possible in a unit in order to maximize the time that I had with them. This involved using very specific language to support this unpacking. For example, I began to use the term 'just right' challenges with my students as part of this process.

Once I shifted my focus and changed key elements of my teaching practice and pedagogy in PE to prioritize the idea of challenge, my teaching really began to take off as I was seeing some amazing student learning in my program.

Setting the scene

The unit I discuss in this chapter is a Grade 5 cycling unit that I have co-taught with other PE teachers at The KAUST School. As all of our students live within our compound at KAUST, we felt that getting our students on bikes would not only build their road safety skills but would also give them more opportunities to explore what is possible by cycling within the KAUST community, where there are multiple paths, roads, and areas that are accessible by bicycle. So our intention throughout this nine-week unit was to provide students with an array of experiences that would provide individualized entry points for riding a bicycle.

Many students were from our host country (Saudi Arabia), and a number of them had limited experiences riding a bicycle. In particular, it was not very common for female students to have experience riding a bicycle at all. Our goal was to change that! Just as I had been inspired by physical activity and sport when I was young, I wanted to inspire every one of our own learners, especially our female students, to experience joy and build their confidence in ways that would motivate them to be risk-takers and curious about what is possible in regard to cycling.

Prioritizing challenge

When designing this unit, we had to plan how we would introduce and unpack the feature of challenge with our students. We wanted to find out what they found to be the most challenging thing when riding their bicycles. Actively involving them from the start of the unit was critical in order to pave the way for them to have **autonomy** and ownership over their learning experiences for the rest of the unit.

By getting students to identify what was most challenging to them, we could then design future lessons that provided them with multiple opportunities to work on what they found to be **personally relevant** and to do so in small groups with their peers in class (**social interaction**). In the event that a student was working alone there were still many opportunities for them to interact with peers. For example, we expected students to show their peers what they were working on and how they had made improvements in their skills.

Another planning consideration was to look at the outdoor space that was available within our school grounds. In the first few classes, we accessed grass pitches, a covered basketball court, multiple paths, rocky surfaces, and sandy surfaces. In the initial assessment of the unit, we simply had students ride their bicycles around the basketball court showing us what they knew about using proper road signals (e.g., stop, left turn, right turn). We could immediately see students who had difficulty with this and worked with them individually and in small groups. After this, students were able to explore different types of surfaces while riding their bicycles around the school grounds.

The most important thing we did was to ensure that we had a driving question to frame the exploration of the school grounds on their bicycles. Our question was: *What are some 'just right' challenges for you when you are riding your bike?*

At the end of the first week of exploration, we had the students share with a partner what they felt their challenges were so far. Students then verbally shared their responses with us, and I jotted their answers in a journal. It was important to capture their thoughts as they were actively involved in co-constructing what challenge meant to them. A strategy we used was to make all learning visible in a poster, which captured what students had told us. By making their ideas visible, the poster became an anchor chart that guided learning over the next several lessons. We added new challenges that were identified to the poster and created secondary posters, as needed, to house these new challenges.

Red, yellow, green dot assessment strategy

Although it was helpful, we found that simply putting up the poster as a talking point was not enough. We had to create conditions for students to self-assess what they were finding challenging. For example, we did not want a student who could barely ride a bicycle to try speeding down a steep hill or to ride quickly in narrow places. We wanted all students to find what they felt were 'just right' entry points or challenges and to practice tasks and skills related to these challenges. Building on the initial posters we developed, the second and third weeks of the unit were focused on continuing the exploration of different challenges but to self-assess using the following sticker scheme:

- Red dot = impossible for me at this point
- Yellow dot = getting there, making some progress
- Green dot = confident, I am able to do this skill well

Working at their own pace, students self-assessed across different cycling skills using the coloured dots as often as possible. They would ride over to the poster and pick out which coloured sticker most applied and then sign their name on the sticker. They put the sticker on the skill they wanted to self-assess, then continued on with their learning. Our hope was that we would begin to see an improvement over time with a student's red dots turning to yellow, then eventually turning to green. Sometimes students would self-assess themselves as a green right away, meaning that they were confident in the skill being assessed. Other times the initial self-assessment was a yellow sticker, meaning that they had a bit of confidence in the skill being assessed but they were not completely confident in their ability.

Moving on up!

After the first three weeks, we felt that students were ready to explore the community on their bikes. We had 45-minute classes, so it was important to get started straight away. There was an area close to the school that we took them to that we felt would offer multiple learning experiences. It was located next to an apartment building complex, so there were parking lots for students to ride their bikes and practice road signals. There were also a variety of gentle slopes, steep dirt hills, rocky areas, and flat areas that consisted of soft sand. All these areas were within 200–300 metres and completely in view of the teachers, so the students could be seen at all times.

Using the red, yellow, and green dot strategy, we also developed pocket sized cards that were red, yellow, and green. Our intention was to get students to *set a goal* for the class. For some students who were still unsteady and unsure of themselves on a bicycle, many set goals to ride around the paved parking lot area practicing road signals. For others, it was riding on the flat, sand-based areas at different speeds (e.g., learning how to shift gears to best suit the terrain they were riding on). And for the more competent riders, they chose to explore riding up and down some of the dirt hills located beside the parking lots. We even had one of our students who was very competent on his bike build ramps in the dirt to practice catching some air – a real risk-taker in action! It was easy to see the smiles, laughter, and the 'Ooos' and 'Ahhhs' of students taking the risks to try new challenges. There was a definite sense of *joy* and engagement in the air. Figure 2.1 shows one example.

It was important that students challenged themselves in an honest way to ensure it was not too easy or difficult. This required a deeper exploration of their skills while also getting the students to consistently self-assess using a 'challenge' assessment scale we had created. As we were now riding outside of the school grounds, the initial poster of challenges that we had created could not be brought with us, so we needed a different way to get the students to self-assess. Our solution was to develop a challenge scale from 1 to 10, where 1 to 4 was green and represented 'Easy Peasy Lemon Squeezy', 5 to 8 was yellow and represented 'Just Right Challenge', and 9 to 10 was red and represented 'Impossible at this Point'.

Developing the challenge scale was one of the most important pedagogical moves we made because it allowed students to self-assess their competence

Figure 2.1 A student cycling on sand

(in relation to challenge) as close to the moment as possible. The prioritized feature of 'challenge' came shining through immediately every single time we sent the students off to explore, to learn, and to discover with their peers (*social interaction*). Being explicit about the challenge scale and getting the students to use the language of the scale was an important pedagogical strategy. We really reinforced the point that a 'just right' challenge meant that they were in the yellow zone between numbers 5–8.

At the end of each class, we came together as a whole group for students to do one final self-assessment (similar to an exit slip; *reflection*).The students showed the number on the challenge scale that represented their self-assessment, and they chose the appropriately coloured card (red, yellow, or green). In one photograph we took of the class you could see 14 of the 17 students in the class being in the yellow zone, which was exactly what we had hoped for.

This process helped students demonstrate a solid understanding of what challenge meant to them in terms of their choice of challenge and the extent to which they were making progress. It was important for us to capture the end of class self-assessment by photo so we could show it to the students in the following class to remind them of how they self-assessed themselves. They were told that they could continue with the same activity or choose something new, but the structure of self-assessment remained in place. If they chose to continue with the same activity and had self-assessed their challenge as being too easy or too difficult, we had a conversation with them about increasing or decreasing the level of challenge. Our goal was to differentiate as much as possible for every student in the class.

As the unit progressed, we stuck with this same assessment structure. By the end of the unit, many students showed a big improvement in their ability to ride a bike and took more risks due to increased confidence.

As a final assessment task, students completed *reflections*, providing them with an opportunity to share what they had learned and how they felt about the cycling unit. The reflection focused on four different areas:

- What was your biggest learning in this unit?
- How did the challenge scale help you in this unit?
- What was your proudest moment in this unit?
- How have you taken action to be a better cyclist in this unit?

Some students wrote about learning hand signals and managing downhill riding. Others also mentioned the ways the challenge scale helped them be 'brave' when approaching hills and developing self-confidence. Clearly this shows how students were developing physical skills but also reveals some emotional competencies.

What have we learned? Where are we going next?

After the unit, we found that many more students were choosing to ride their bikes to and from school each day, which was evidence to us that cycling had become more a part of their identity and suggested that they had found cycling to be personally relevant beyond PE. Some other things we learned include:

1) Through conversations with and observations of students, prioritizing the feature of 'challenge' had a positive impact on student learning in the cycling unit. This was reinforced through our formal assessment practices. Some students made huge gains while others seemed to definitely get better and find more joy in cycling. In particular, we had a number of local Saudi female students who had barely ridden a bicycle before the unit, and they developed much more confidence in themselves as evidenced by their improved ability on the bicycle and willingness to push themselves to get better.

2) Although the red, yellow, and green dot assessment strategy worked well, we felt that we could be more precise in the way the students self-assessed using this strategy to show a layering of dots rather than having them randomly placed. We made a change to get the students to sign off on a coloured dot then place it on the challenge poster so it overlapped with one of their previous dot assessments. This allowed students and the teacher to see how they felt that they had progressed in the unit in relation to the challenges they had chosen to explore. For example, a student who may have assessed themselves as red (impossible at this point) might go away and practice whatever it was they chose to focus on and then re-assess themselves later in the class or the following class. If they had turned to a yellow, they used the yellow sticker and overlapped it with the previous red sticker. After more practice, they might turn to a green (confident and able) sticker. They would then place the green sticker so it overlapped with the previous red and yellow stickers. This was a great way to see their progress in the unit.

3) I wanted to align an after-school cycling club with the cycling unit in PE. The hope was that we would get some of the students who were excited and inspired about cycling to join the after-school cycling club. Although the club was small due to the teacher-student ratio (only one teacher running the club), we had a few other Grade 5 students join. Two were local Saudi female students who, at the beginning of the cycling unit, had struggled with their skills. They had a basic level of ability riding a bicycle but kept practicing their skills in PE and in the after-school cycling club. Both of the students made a big improvement

Figure 2.2 A sense of joy while cycling

in their ability. One student even convinced her father to buy her a new bike halfway through the unit. By the end of the unit in PE and the after-school cycling club, she was challenging herself in many different ways including riding off-road up and down bigger hills and racing with other students. The photo in Figure 2.2 shows this student in the middle of the unit. Notice the huge smile on her face!

What can we do better?

Although we felt the unit was well-structured and the students seemed to really enjoy it, there were areas that could be improved. Bike safety remains a critically important aspect of this unit. There are some students who are simply not ready to venture out into the community with the rest of the class due to a limited ability to ride safely on the roads. These students can often hold the class back from getting to where we need to go. We are rethinking the way we run the cycling classes to keep some students back at the school to work on the basics of safety, while the others who demonstrate more responsibility on the roads can leave the school to explore cycling in the community.

Level 1, level 2, level 3 challenges

We felt that another important change was to be clearer on the types of challenges and in some cases, making all students start with a level 1 challenge. This would be the easiest form of the challenge. They could then progress to level 2 and then level three challenges. We began to use this language with students to help them better articulate the level of challenge. For example, if the students were working on riding up and down hills, it would be a requirement that they start on the easiest hill first. If they assessed themselves as a 'green' (Easy Peasy Lemon Squeezy) they would have to do a level 1 challenge at least three times before being able to advance to a level 2 challenge, which in this case would be a hill that is steeper. They would then have to ride this level 2 hill at least three times showing competence before moving to a level 3 hill (most advanced).

We felt that breaking down the difficulty into level 1, level 2, and level 3 challenges helped to build confidence but in a safe progression rather than going for the most difficult challenges straight away.

Wrapping up

Although I have focused this chapter on our cycling unit, we have also used the Meaningful PE approach (with a prioritization on the feature of 'challenge'), in two other units (individual pursuits with a focus on skateboarding and a racquet sports unit). We have noticed some patterns emerge regarding student learning in these units.

1) Engagement was high in the unit due to our students being able to identify what was most challenging for them and through *voice and choice* being able to focus on developing the skills they wanted to get better at.
2) Students (mostly) self-assessed themselves honestly and chose the 'just right' challenges that best suited them. Although there were times when they lost focus, it was easy to redirect them based on the work we had done in prioritizing challenge and getting students to understand what a 'just right' challenge was for them in the unit.
3) Behaviour management issues dropped significantly as most students were able to access learning in a way that kept them engaged for longer periods of time in class lessons. However, there were still students with high needs and with serious behaviour management issues. These students needed specific interventions and more teacher direction. Figuring out how to include them in our rides in the community has been a struggle and has led to discussion about how to separate groups. For the students who are unable to ride in the community, they must stay

back at school. This means that we need extra adult supervision at the school as the rest of the students are out in the community exploring their riding skills. In some cases, the students with higher needs might be able to ride in the community but need one-to-one support. Working out these issues is an important part of the planning process in the cycling unit.

As I continue to teach using ideas from Meaningful PE, I am excited to further explore what is possible in terms of student learning in PE. I have connected with a group of like-minded practitioners who are equally passionate about the Meaningful PE approach and work with them to continually push the boundaries, experiment, and refine the approaches that we are using in order to deepen student learning in PE. Although it has been an exciting journey of learning and discovery, there is still so much that is unknown to us. Therefore, we must stay committed to the process of finding out and to being open to the critical feedback needed to continually improve our practice so that we can offer the most meaningful learning experiences possible for our students in PE.

3 Meaningful Physical Education with immigrant newcomers

Milena Trojanovic

Introduction

I have been a primary/elementary health and physical education (H&PE) teacher for 28 years, working in a public school board in Ontario, Canada. I spent my first 23 years at a school where I grew deep roots and developed strong relationships within the community surrounding the school; at times, I taught the children of parents whom I had previously taught. Through those years I had also taken on a variety of teaching-related experiences, working on curriculum development and professional learning initiatives within my school board and across the province. In 2015 an opportunity to teach in a new school presented itself, and I felt this might offer me a new challenge. Since then, I have had the role of lead H&PE teacher in this new school. My teaching partner and I teach 1200 students in Grades 1–8 for 40–60 minutes, twice a week. The school is located in a rapidly growing suburban area, where many students and their families are immigrant newcomers to Canada and represent diverse social and cultural backgrounds.

Upon first arriving at the school, I thought my experience meant I would be well prepared to develop and teach a quality H&PE program. For example, I thought I would be able to transfer how I drew from students' background knowledge and abilities to offer both traditional and non-traditional H&PE experiences. I had come from a school and community where teachers could assume students had a strong basis for fundamental skills. I was now at a place where these assumptions did not hold. My teaching partner and I realized we needed to adopt a different approach that better reflected our learners – their experiences, abilities, and interests – and that supported them in seeing how H&PE could be an important part of their lives.

Why Meaningful PE for me and my students?

My philosophy for teaching H&PE has been to provide students with the building blocks to be successful movers so they can apply their skills to experience *joy* and find lifelong opportunities for healthy movement and activity. The reference to joy in my philosophy aligns with some of the main ideas underpinning the Meaningful PE approach.

I always felt that students who had an inclination for physical activities were not my main target audience, as I assumed that they would likely succeed in all aspects of an H&PE program when given the chance to perform. My focus has therefore been on those who need more attention and multiple opportunities for success through various and non-traditional H&PE content and pedagogies. Helping students learn to love to move based on positive *social interactions* has shaped much of my teaching.

My philosophy has not always been as it is now. Early in my career, I mostly followed colleagues who felt that teaching traditional sports and completing fitness tests (including posting students' results) was *the* way to deliver an H&PE program. In those early years I recalled how I was inspired by my own H&PE teacher who knew that traditional sports were not for everyone. I too was a child of immigrant parents, and in my family, sports were one of the last things we were encouraged to focus on as first-generation Canadians. As I became more comfortable and confident in my teaching, I began to question what it was that I and others were doing. I knew there must be better, more effective ways to meet the needs of all learners. I began to learn about and teach using Teaching Games for Understanding (TGfU); its inquiry- and student-centred nature was exactly what I felt would help support my philosophy and desire to improve the quality of my students' H&PE experiences. At that point I felt I had found my niche and I was able to offer a more solid program for all students.

In the last few years, I have become familiar with the Meaningful PE approach, which has been intriguing based on my personal and professional background but also because it has offered me a new way to think about how I engage my students. I have always been a reflective practitioner. In thinking through what Meaningful PE was about, it seemed to be a natural extension of much of what I was already doing. For example, I could still teach using approaches like TGfU while tailoring them more closely to what students found meaningful in their experience. It also provided me with a sense of validation that things like joy and meaningfulness were important to the quality of an H&PE program and to the quality of students' lives.

Using Meaningful PE to guide planning and teaching decisions in gymnastics

The Meaningful PE approach offered me a way to become clearer in how I shared my thoughts with students about the 'why, what, and how' of the things we are doing in H&PE. Over the first few years at my new school I had been challenged to express these thoughts with students, given the difference in their backgrounds and experiences compared to those I had taught previously. This clearly captures the challenges I faced in trying to ensure that H&PE was personally relevant for students. In implementing the Meaningful PE approach, the feature of *personally relevant learning* became a clear focus for my teaching. Through paying attention to personally relevant learning and several of the other features of Meaningful PE, I felt that I could provide a rich set of learning experiences that enabled students to see how H&PE could improve the quality of their lives.

In the spring of 2019, I modified a unit for gymnastics that was designed to help students develop confidence in their movement capabilities. I have experienced how educational gymnastics (rather than Olympic gymnastics) provides students with opportunities to solve problems and explore the functional qualities of movement. There are also several expectations (or outcomes) in the Ontario H&PE curriculum that align well with educational gymnastics tasks and activities. Because gymnastics was new to many students, I had to offer exciting opportunities to engage in experiences that were quite novel and appealing, and that allowed them to interact with others in positive ways (*fun, social interaction*). As mentioned, however, one of the challenges I had was helping students to see the personal relevance of gymnastics, that is, to understand how they could take aspects of their experience in gymnastics to apply to their lives outside of school.

The general outline of the three-week unit in educational gymnastics is presented in Table 3.1:

Table 3.1 Outline of gymnastics unit tasks

Week	Key tasks
1	Introduction and safety; balance (e.g., points/patches, traditional static balances, partner stunts)
2	Jumping, landing, pathways, travelling. Different surfaces and apparatus (e.g., floor, benches, mats and benches, obstacle courses to improve stability). Transfer of weight, including rotations.
3	Putting it all together with balances, travelling, jumping and landing, rotations

While the outline in Table 3.1 provided a general structure for the unit and lessons, there were developmentally appropriate modifications made for students in each grade and class.

To start the unit, I engaged students in a discussion about the 'why' of gymnastics: how gymnastics could help them develop skills that were important both within and beyond the walls of the gym (*personal relevance; reflection*). For example, we discussed the benefits of building stability for a variety of activities they might be doing in the playground or elsewhere in the community. Safety was also at the forefront of my planning and decision-making, as no one was having *fun* if they were getting hurt or not feeling safe. I thought that if they could learn how to be safe in our class, they might see the ***personal relevance*** of these experiences for learning how to be safe in movement experiences outside of school. In each class we reinforced the rules of safety and added more depending on the activity. For example, once we taught safe jumping and landing, we introduced benches as apparatus and stressed the importance of someone always sitting on the end to ensure they did not tip; we taught active spotting for people whose bodies were off the ground during pyramid building opportunities; we reminded them of the removal of glasses, hard headbands, and hijab pins when rolling. This provided a foundation to introduce students to some important learning opportunities and experiences they might engage in for the remainder of the unit.

At the beginning of each lesson, we introduced a movement learning goal as well as social goals (***motor competence, social interaction, goal-setting***). In making these explicit, it was my intention to help students become aware of the *reasons* behind why we were asking them to engage in specific tasks and to help them draw connections between how these things might be relevant to broader aspects of their lives (***personally relevant learning***). Many of the movement goals were framed around stability and balancing, moving their bodies in smooth and controlled ways, and considering how to solve problems and explore movement using the concepts of body, space, effort, and relationships. The social goals were mostly to ensure they included their classmates, respected ability levels, and used positive words to encourage others (***social interaction***). In our school, we use the 'Work Hard, Be Nice, and Make a Difference' motto to frame all that we do, making it easy to remind or inquire if students are (or are not) working hard, being nice or making a difference. For example, we ask them to ensure that no one is left in 'lost and found' (a place where students can go if they feel isolated). Typically, the students do not fear going to the lost and found area (in the middle of the gym usually with a teacher standing there) because they know someone will come to their rescue. We like to allow for some flexibility when making groups and will give students choice at times (***autonomy***), while at others we use creative ways of making groups.

In Table 3.2, I include some other strategies embedded in the Meaningful PE approach beyond what I have described earlier. These were selected based on their alignment with the features of Meaningful PE.

As shown in Table 3.2, many planning and teaching decisions that aligned readily with one feature of Meaningful PE also linked with others. For example, several of the strategies used to focus on movement competence also provided opportunities for students to experience optimal

Table 3.2 Using the Features of Meaningful PE to support planning and teaching decisions

Social Interaction

- Provide opportunities for students to work by themselves, with a partner or in small groups
- Use an 'elbow partner' to turn and talk to (*reflection*)
- When students are not comfortable performing certain tasks (e.g., human pyramid), have alternative roles and contributions to allow for success (e.g., active spotter)
- Acknowledge when students make positive comments or show respect to one another
- Celebrate those who are: working hard and trying new challenges, safely on task
- Provide opportunities for students who have prior knowledge and experiences to demonstrate *movement competence* and model for the class
- Take photos for the class website to foster inclusion and build lasting memories

Fun

- Provide novel and creative opportunities for engagement in non-traditional activity (gymnastics).
- Provide choices based on comfort level to ensure activity is fun and safe (*autonomy*)
- Offer a "Daily Fun Challenge" as a warm-up using fun activities
- Reduce interpersonal competition
- Ask students what they found fun about their experience and why (*reflection*)

Challenge

- Encourage students to find their 'Goldilocks' level of challenge: 'not too hard, not too easy, just right'. For example, provide differentiated opportunities for students to attempt stability challenges (*autonomy*).
- Use *reflection and goal-setting* to identify appropriate levels of challenge
- Remind students that everyone has their own comfort for activity, and various levels of challenge will be offered so all needs can be met.
- Offer different forms of *interaction* to adjust the level of challenge (e.g., individual, partner, group, active spotters) (*autonomy*)
- Celebrate personal accomplishment related to challenge (e.g., a student wants to share something they mastered or if a group would like to share a performance or sequence)

Movement Competence

- Demonstrate balances and transfers of weight (such as rotations). Ask students to demonstrate if they feel comfortable.
- Model both 'example' and 'non-example'
- Acknowledge the importance of trying new skills and taking risks (*challenge*) but not at the expense of their own safety or that of others
- Encourage students to complete tasks (obstacle courses, skills stations) at their own personal comfort level (*autonomy*)
- Offer support to master skills if students seek help (e.g., help primary students do front roll by being active spotters for them)

(Continued)

Table 3.2 (Continued)

Personally Relevant Learning

- Help students make connections between gymnastics and their lives outside of school through questioning and providing opportunities for critical and creative thinking
- Show a video of gymnasts in the Olympics or PanAm Games to excite them for learning possibilities (***goal-setting***)
- Complete oral exit passes with specific questions that relate to the personal relevance of the learning (e.g., What did you learn today that you could use somewhere else?) (***reflection***)

---

levels of challenge. Also, by focusing on one or more of the features in my planning I could see how ***student autonomy*** could be supported, or how approaches such as ***reflection and goal-setting*** could engage students in a particular task or experience.

As explained earlier in the chapter, one of the main challenges I was presented with in working with students at my school – not only in gymnastics but across many parts of the program – was to make H&PE personally relevant to them. Being explicit about how students could apply some of what they were learning offered one way of doing this. However, the main approach I used was simply to ask them about the connections they were making based on their experiences. Over the years I have tried to make the connections for students myself, but during this unit I was intent on asking *them* about the personal relevance of their experiences. Using targeted ***reflective questions*** about the relevance they were finding in their learning and asking students for feedback was a different approach that a focus on Meaningful PE provided me with, and I appreciated that most students were able to make connections independently.

While I cannot present actual quotes from my students due to ethical reasons, in the following passages I show how I used the language of the Ontario H&PE curriculum and of Meaningful PE to develop questions that supported students in seeing the personal relevance of their gymnastics experience. The responses I offer are paraphrased and drawn from my teaching notes, but they provide authentic representations of the experiences of several students across various grade levels. It is also interesting to note the ways several students used the language of the features of Meaningful PE in their responses.

Q: How can building confidence using your body in different ways influence how you participate in physical activities in the future?

- *It can help me when I go to the park and play on the climber. I can be strong, and I can be brave and try something new.* (Grade 1 response)

- *I can jump across rocks and not fall down.* (Grade 4 response)
- *I know that I get more confident with trying new things, and then I can feel better and be stronger and healthier.* (Grade 6 response)
- *I can develop strength and improve my core muscles, and I can be more flexible so that I don't injure myself in the future.* (Grade 7 response)

Q: What kinds of things make this activity enjoyable for you as a participant?

- *I like that there was lots to do, and we got to move everywhere and use our bodies differently.* (Grade 2 response)
- *I enjoyed being able to work with lots of people to make the pyramids work, and I like that I was able to try a hard challenge like the bunk bed roll.* (Grade 7 response)
- *It was just fun.* (Grade 7 response)
- *I enjoyed working on the different challenges, collaborating and trying new things.* (Grade 8 response)
- *I think that this type of activity lets someone discover themselves. . . . For example, I might not believe I can accomplish something, but I set a goal and I was successful. It is like that when you become an adult and try to do something new.* (Grade 8 response)

Q: How might what we learned today help you in your lives? For example, what safety considerations do you need to consider here in the gym as well as in other environments, and how can we connect our learning to something we might want to do in the future?

- *I know that if I am safe by doing only the things that I feel comfortable doing, then I will know what I can do if I am at a park or a recreation centre and still be safe with my friends.* (Grade 7 response)
- *I learned who I can trust, and maybe in the future I can approach those people if I need to talk to someone or if I need help with something.* (Grade 8 response)

A reflection on using the Meaningful PE approach

I like the Meaningful PE approach and see this fitting naturally into how I teach. Ultimately the success of my teaching is about each child and how I can make each learning experience a positive one for them. The gymnastics unit was successful in that student engagement was excellent considering that we taught over 1000 students, many of whom did not have a lot of prior knowledge or experiences with gymnastics. Students experienced a wide and appropriate level of *challenge* (e.g., they could choose to use the mats on the floor, aerobic steps, and/or benches as they mastered their skills for balances, rotations, jumping/landing, and traveling). Once we taught the safety and the progression of skills through carefully planned lessons, the students were able to comfortably and safely explore their own challenges and find *delight* in being successful and engaging with their peers. In addition, they were able to clearly articulate which activities they enjoyed and why, and how these opportunities could help them in the future by making personally relevant connections. When I engaged Grade 7/8 students in a reflective discussion about their experience for the first day using a 'finger flash' (with four fingers being the best and one finger being terrible), not one student in all eight Grade 7/8 classes flashed me less than three fingers, with most being four. When I asked them to provide a reason, almost all of them said it was *fun* to build pyramids and they enjoyed working on something different with their friends in the classes, especially since they all had a role (whether it was being a part of the actual structure or whether they were active spotters). They felt they accomplished physical feats by cooperating and trusting each other. I was amazed at how they were able to identify the importance of trust and how it would apply to them in the future.

It has always been my hope that there is some connection made by students for future reference, but this approach has definitely made me more aware of the importance of being intentional in my delivery. I do like that all of the features seem to work together, and even though I might plan explicitly for *fun*, it won't be all that fun without the *social interaction* being positive or the *challenge* being in the 'Goldilocks' zone of 'just right'. The pieces all fit together quite well and work in sync with one another.

I will continue to use the Meaningful PE approach in the future with the students I teach at my school. Being intentional about prioritizing meaningful experiences is important to help students make connections and create meaningfulness for them in the long term. Although student voice was not an option for some parts of this unit due to safety reasons, there were still many opportunities for students to have *choice* in their challenges. Student engagement was increased when there were multiple choices for them to try. This approach encouraged risk-taking in safe ways and helped foster positive student interaction when skills were mastered.

I would like to use a more formalized *reflection* for the older students in the future. I feel that this would be an ideal chance for them to do some writing based on some of their own personally relevant learning as well as provide an opportunity for them to set and track *goals* for participation and build connections that are deeper and more meaningful. In addition, I feel that giving the primary students more of an opportunity to discuss the 'what, how, why' of learning might be something that would bring another layer of meaningfulness for them. I find I am more explicit with junior and intermediate students (Grades 4–8), and I perhaps neglect this element with the primary classes (Grades 1–3). There was one 'aha' moment when I had rushed to get all the safety and instructions done quickly so that Grade 2 students could begin exploring an obstacle course. In the middle of the class, a student asked: 'Why are we learning this?' I realized I had been doing a disservice to the primary students by not being explicit about this. I told her to go and try the challenges and then tell me what she thought at the end of the class. As part of the cool down, I asked the students: 'Why do you suppose we did activities like this today and how might this help you when you grow up?' A very eager hand shot up quickly to answer before the rest of the class had a chance to think about the question: 'We had a lot of fun with our friends trying to move our bodies in different ways so that we could be balanced and stronger, plus we had to wait our turn sometimes'. I certainly learned my lesson and it was a 'delightful' moment on my part to know that even my youngest students could make connections that were meaningful to them given the chance to explore and discover ways to move in a *fun* way.

4 Committing to the idea of Meaningful Physical Education in teaching practice

Stephanie Beni

Introduction

I was first introduced to the idea of meaningfulness in PE as an undergraduate student in a university PE course. At the same time, I was privileged to have a position teaching PE in a small private school for primary/elementary and high school students in Ontario. I was immediately intrigued by the idea of meaningfulness both for my studies and for my teaching practice. Of course, I wanted my students to find meaning in what I was teaching them; however, knowing *how* to do that was another story. Shortly after I completed the university course, I began working on the Learning About Meaningful Physical Education (LAMPE) project as a research assistant while also completing my undergraduate thesis where I conducted a self-study of my practice of trying to answer the question of 'how' to promote meaningful experiences for my students in PE. I used the features of Meaningful PE as a starting point to guide my pedagogical decision-making, intentionally prioritizing the presence of the features in each lesson. While that particular research project was only eight weeks long, it has had a lasting impact on my teaching practice.

I am now a PhD student continuing to work toward a better understanding of how we can promote meaningfulness for students in PE. My doctoral research has provided me with the opportunity to work with several other PE teachers who have the same passion for improving their teaching and from whom I have learned much. At the same time, I have continued to teach school-based PE. Over the past several years, I have endeavoured to continue informally studying my own practice, writing reflections on critical incidents that have stood out in relation to Meaningful PE and my changing perceptions of how to plan for and implement it. I have also leaned quite heavily on student feedback to determine if my efforts to prioritize meaningfulness are both explicit and impactful to them.

As I reflect on nearly five years of aiming to prioritize meaningfulness in my teaching practice, two things in particular stand out to me as being critical. First, it has required a commitment to the ***idea of meaningfulness***, particularly in terms of allowing students the time necessary to enter their personal playgrounds, as Kretchmar (2006) suggests. This has taken time, effort, a great deal of reflection, the challenging of my own assumptions about teaching and learning, a willingness to allow others to observe my practice and provide feedback, and a commitment to staying current on what other researchers and teachers are saying on the topic. In other words, it has been (and continues to be) an ongoing professional learning project for me. Second, in addition to my own commitment to prioritizing meaningfulness, I have worked hard to share the responsibility of this task with my students to help them see the important role they play in this process. Over the years, my students and I have aimed to use the ***features*** of Meaningful PE as a ***shared language*** to help us become more reflective of the factors that are influencing the meaningfulness of our experiences.

It is my aim in this chapter to use a few illustrative examples from my teaching practice over the past few years to demonstrate how and why these two key principles (committing to the idea of meaningfulness and sharing the responsibility with students) have become pillars to me and why Meaningful PE will stay at the core of my teaching vision for years to come.

Committing to Meaningful PE

When I began working with and learning from other teachers, I quickly realized my personal conception of Meaningful PE was quite narrow in that it was derived largely from studying my own practice. As I observed the ways other teachers were teaching and implementing ideas about meaningfulness in their classrooms, I began to question some of my own practices. That was not problematic or bothersome to me at all; I have tried to always stay open to challenging my perspectives in an effort to learn and grow. As I discussed ideas about Meaningful PE with other teachers, I began to ask myself why I was doing things the way I was, not as a matter of determining whose way was 'right', but to ask myself if what I was doing was really best for *my* students in *my* classroom. For example, I had committed myself to focusing on a few long units of study in PE as opposed to trying to cover a whole lot of content in a short period of time – wanting to avoid the issues of enacting a curriculum that was a mile wide but an inch deep. This decision was made based upon my commitment to the prioritization of meaningfulness for my students. As I filtered my pedagogical decision-making through the features and the framework of Meaningful PE, I felt that longer, more in-depth units were more likely to promote meaningfulness. For instance, I felt there was no way my students could possibly become ***competent*** in any particular skill or activity in just a few short lessons. While I was not aiming to produce Olympic-level athletes, I was conscious that motor competence was a key factor in students' willingness to continue to be active. I also wanted my students to be ***challenged***, but also to have adequate time to ***set goals*** toward and overcome those challenges. I felt these things required and were worth an investment of time.

While I felt so sure this was the right thing to do, I began to question this assumption based on what I was observing and hearing from other teachers. This led me to try something new with my students. At the end of the previous school year, I had tried to do some jump rope activities with them, and if I am really being honest, it failed quite miserably. We had a very short period of time (about three weeks), and some of the older boys in particular, were just 'too cool' for jump rope. I abandoned the idea in response to the negativity and decided it would be unlikely we would return. However, the very next school year, being reinvigorated by a presentation I had seen at a PE workshop, along with a double-dutch scene from a movie that many of my students had come to love, I decided to dive headlong into jump rope again, committing wholeheartedly to spending a lot of time here with my students. I would use it as a test, I told myself, in the midst of my uncertainty.

The first lesson was rough, to say the least. However, I quickly started using the ***features*** of Meaningful PE to evaluate my decisions and make adjustments (and to encourage my students to do the same). Within a few short lessons, I could tell my students were really getting into it. I made sure that our lessons had a focus on building the fitness and coordination necessary to do some of the cool 'tricks' students were keen to learn (developing ***motor competence***). However, I was careful not to push them too far. I did this by allowing them to choose from several options (***challenge; autonomy***). For instance, I might demonstrate five tricks and ask them to work toward being able to perform any three of them – giving them the opportunity to choose their level of challenge. In this way, every student was able to be successful. I also really wanted to make jump rope ***fun*** – so, of course, this involved lots of music (I am also the music teacher), playing jump rope games, and offering free time at the end of each class to work either with a partner, small group, or solo on something related to what we had learned that day or to build their fitness through jump rope games (***autonomy, social interaction***). During this time, students were also given the opportunity to work toward some optional 'preset' ***challenges*** I had created (e.g., continuous jumping for a fixed amount of time). I was surprised to see how many students took these on and really challenged themselves.

After the first few lessons, parents and students began to report back to me that they had gone out (at their child's request) to purchase a jump rope for home; they began to see it as a useful and enjoyable form of physical activity that they wished to carry with them beyond the classroom (***personally relevant learning***). As we worked our way through the unit, I suggested that we might perform a whole-class culminating jump sequence (similar to the aforementioned movie scene they were quite keen on) to which they could invite their parents. My students were quick to agree and eagerly took full initiative to organize, plan, practice for, assign (and complete) homework tasks toward, and invite their guests to this event (***autonomy***, ***student-centred learning***). While there were undoubtedly challenges that arose as students took on roles and shared their opinions, I encouraged students to use this as an opportunity to work on some critical social skills (***social interaction***) and to draw their attention to how these skills might be helpful in other areas of their lives (***personally relevant learning***).

My students' initiative during this project was a teacher's dream come true. Yet this nagging sense in the back of my mind that we really 'should' move along so we could cover more units of content had me continually suggesting to students that we might spend just one more lesson on this activity. However, my students were quick to tell me that this would not be enough time to get their tricks just right, and so we continued with the unit (***student voice***). Our jump rope unit ended up spanning two full months (with two one-hour physical education periods each week). While I understand that for many teachers (here in Ontario at least) this would be quite challenging given curricular and administrative objectives and requirements, it was the perfect thing for my students.

Before the end of the unit, I received feedback from students about how much they had enjoyed the experience of learning to jump rope, including specific comments in relation to the amount of time we spent on the unit allowing them the opportunity to develop the skills and stamina needed to feel confident (***motor competence***) and to feel as though they could articulate something they had learned (***personally relevant learning***). Through this experience I began to see that my commitment to doing what I felt would facilitate a meaningful movement experience for my students was the right choice, even though it was daunting in the beginning and was even challenging for my students at times. Importantly, I was also able to recognize that this might *not* be the right choice for other teachers in other contexts and that that was okay.

The decisions I was making along the way, in terms of *what* to teach, *how* to teach, and *how long* to teach this particular activity were guided by my commitment to prioritizing meaningfulness through the Meaningful PE approach. In moments of doubt, uncertainty, or tension, I returned to the features and the pedagogies of Meaningful PE and looked for ways to bring about positive change. I have written elsewhere (Beni, Fletcher, & Ní

Chróinín, 2019) of a similar experience with learning to navigate how much emphasis to place on competition in PE, ultimately allowing my focus on meaningfulness through the Meaningful PE approach to guide the decisions I have made. This process has never failed me and is why prioritizing meaningfulness has become the core of my vision for teaching PE. That is not to say that we have not had challenging days or lessons in PE, but rather that my students and I have learned to work through it *together* as we stay committed to prioritizing meaningfulness (though we still have so much to learn).

Sharing the responsibility

While my own commitment to the idea of promoting meaningfulness has been central to my continued professional learning, equally important has been the realization that my students play a crucial role in this process and that I simply *cannot* facilitate meaningful experiences *for* them. On the contrary, it is something I have learned we must do together. Thus, one of the most significant challenges I have faced on this journey has been learning to share that responsibility (and a *sense* of responsibility) with my students.

In addition to teaching PE, I also coach our students in preparation for regional cross-country running events in both the fall and spring of each school year. I have always been challenged as a teacher/coach to prioritize and facilitate meaningful experiences in running, mostly because students often seem to not enjoy it much. Personally, I get quite a thrill out of the challenge of training for a long-distance race. However, transferring that joy to my students has proven quite difficult.

Recently, in preparation for one such event, as the weather was turning warm and the fields were beginning to dry up, I took my students out for a nice run – nothing too long, but something to get them back out there after the long winter months. Suffice to say, there were some complaints. I wanted to use the opportunity to generate **reflection** on how we might apply what we know about meaningfulness to the situation. I began to ask students if the experience, in general, had been very meaningful. Unsurprisingly, the response was no. I responded by asking what we were going to do about that. I think students were initially taken aback that I had put some of the responsibility for this on them; they seemed unsure that there was anything that could be done about it. I probed a bit further and asked them to use the features of meaningful experiences (**shared language**) and really **reflect** on whether there was anything that could be done about it. Together we began talking through some of the different features to identify what was missing: How could we aim for a 'just right' level of **challenge**? Could we add a **social** element that might make the process more enjoyable? Was there a way to work this into or make connections to other areas of their lives (***personally relevant learning***)? Having reflected upon these, I put out a challenge asking students to consider putting together a plan for how they could experience meaningfulness in running. It was not homework. It was not mandatory. It was simply a suggestion. It was interesting to watch the ways different students responded to this, some of whom took the challenge up and (quite literally) ran with it, using the features to help guide the development of plans that could be implemented not only at school but also at home to build stamina and find ways to enjoy running. I later received feedback from both students and parents about what an enjoyable running experience this situation had turned out to be.

This experience, and others like it, challenged my perception of what 'teaching' should look like. Realistically, I did very little to help my students find meaningfulness in running apart from using our ***shared language*** and other pedagogies of Meaningful PE to guide them toward finding personal significance in movement on their own. In addition to the challenges *I* have faced as a teacher, my students have also been challenged by learning to take responsibility for the meaningfulness of their experiences, largely through exercising more ***autonomy***. Students' socialization into the experience of 'school' has often taught them that the teacher should be the transmitter of knowledge and they should simply listen and do as they are asked. To illustrate, recently, I was asking students for suggestions on something we were co-planning. Some of the students made suggestions that were contrary to the way I had been doing things. I simply said, 'okay,' and began to work toward incorporating their feedback. Some of my students said it felt 'weird' to make a suggestion to the teacher and have the teacher say, 'okay.' There seemed to be a sense that they were 'telling me what to do' and that that was contrary to how school was supposed to work. I used this moment as an opportunity to share with the class that I wanted them to feel free to make suggestions and share their ideas so we could all learn together. In spite of having taught many of these students for several years, and though I can see how they have grown tremendously in their willingness to take responsibility for their own learning, this has been one of my greatest challenges in attempting to prioritize meaningfulness for and with them.

One day, as we were preparing for class in a track and field unit, I asked students to work together in small groups to prepare a skill development station, each of which should be related to a unique skill/activity we would be working on that day. After students had created their station, they would take a few moments to explain it to the other groups and then cycle around completing each station. I asked students to remember how important ***challenge*** is to them and their peers when creating meaningful movement opportunities and suggested they should design their stations in a way that would allow others to choose (***autonomy***) from several levels of challenge.

After sending students to complete this task, I walked around listening to their conversations and observing how they were setting up their stations. I noticed they seemed to be struggling with setting varying levels of challenge; they were hesitant to provide too many options as students who were more skilled could potentially choose something that would be too easy for them. They discussed possibly providing different levels of challenge but making 'rules' about who could and could not choose each one. I stopped them for a moment and had a chat with them about having the freedom to make choices for ourselves and the way I had prioritized that in my teaching practice with them to help make things more meaningful (***autonomy***). We discussed the fact that when we allow others to make choices for themselves, sometimes we risk that people may not make the 'right' choice, or what we *think* is the right choice, but that allowing people the freedom to do so is an important thing to preserve. We were able to connect this to other areas of life in which we might disagree but must respect people's choices (***personally relevant learning***). I encouraged them to set a few options and let others choose, and they did.

As students cycled through the stations, I watched to see how many students chose the 'easy' level when they could have or maybe should have chosen a more difficult version of the task. Not one student did. Afterward I followed up with students (***reflection***) and asked what they had noticed. They too had realized that their peers made appropriate choices for themselves when given the opportunity to do so. While it was an important lesson for my students, perhaps it had an even bigger impact on me. I began to ask myself how many times I still do what my students were doing in this scenario. While I undoubtedly believe, as Dewey (1938) suggests, that student-centred learning does not mean leaving students to their own devices but requires guidance from the teacher, I have also come to realize that my students are quite capable of rising to new heights when given the opportunity. I simply *cannot* prioritize meaningful experiences *for* them *without* them. Recognizing that the process is a shared responsibility has been one of the most important, and yet most challenging, realizations to work toward. Yet the closer we get to functioning as partners in learning, the more I realize that it is worth it.

Conclusion

I certainly do not mean to suggest that all of our PE classes and experiences are neat and tidy or meaningful. Often, I am certain my classroom looks a bit like a zoo, and some days I would like nothing more than to roll out a ball, walk out, and let students sort it out themselves. However, in those moments, I ask my students (and myself) to go back to the features and pedagogies of Meaningful PE and figure out where we are missing it. In our most recent unit, in which we spent several weeks on creative dance, there were moments when I felt the only logical thing to do was to just call it a wrap and move along. However, as we used the features together to assess where we were going wrong, we were able to bring about positive changes that helped to make it a worthwhile endeavour for all.

The more I learn about prioritizing meaningfulness with my students, the more I realize just how much I do not yet know. However, as I have stayed committed to the concept of prioritizing meaningfulness through the Meaningful PE approach and have worked with my students to share that responsibility with them, I have learned so much. I have seen my experiences and those of my students transformed in such a way that I have no intention of ever returning to whatever it was we were doing before we began prioritizing meaningfulness.

Importantly, I acknowledge that my perception of meaningfulness has, to this point, focused largely around the idea of the features of Meaningful PE (and particularly how my students experience those features in our own context). As a way forward, it is my aim to broaden these horizons and not be limited by what may be a fairly narrow conception of meaningfulness and the factors that may influence it. In particular, I have found that sharing ideas with other teachers who share my passion for moving toward meaningfulness with their students has helped me to challenge my assumptions and open to up to new ideas. I still have a lot to learn, but what an amazing (and meaningful) journey it continues to be!

References

Beni, S., Fletcher, T., & Ní Chróinín, D. (2019). Using features of meaningful experiences to guide primary physical education practice. *European Physical Education Review*, *25*, 599–615.

Dewey, J. (1938). *Experience and education*. New York, NY: Macmillan Publishing Co.

Kretchmar, R. S. (2006). Ten more reasons for quality physical education. *Journal of Physical Education, Recreation and Dance*, *77*(9), 6–9.

5   Meaningful PE as a metaphor for teaching PE

Alex Beckey

Introduction

After more than a decade of teaching PE, I had what Tripp (1993) would class as a 'critical incident'. A train journey provided me a serendipitous meeting with an ex-student of mine, who proceeded to offer an honest and heartfelt evaluation of my teaching and its impact on him. My unrelenting pursuit of technical mastery through the constant repetition of isolated practice, hyper-corrective feedback that always pointed out deficiencies, and manipulative emotional outbursts had sucked out any delight he may have found in PE and school sport.

This critical incident was the catalyst for a profound personal and professional reflection on the place movement has to play in enriching an individual's life and PE's role in promoting that. This reflection is ongoing and continues to shape my thinking and interactions within my role. In the last five years of my teaching career I have found the Meaningful PE approach and the ideas of Kretchmar (2005) and Metheny (1968) helpful in guiding my judgements and actions to ensure that history does not repeat itself.

PE teachers who, like me, subscribe to the creation of meaningful experiences for learners are influenced not just by the achievement of learning objectives but by the value the learner attributes to all forms of movement and to PE itself. Our professional judgement and decision-making can be guided by *features* of meaningful experiences. Within PE this can be done practically in two significant ways: by the teacher's reflection on- and in-action.

According to Schön (1983), a teacher's reflection on-action involves careful attention to what has occurred after a lesson, unit, or year of teaching. If a PE Department has a clear, shared vision of what PE should entail and what it can offer, that vision can be used as a filter for an individual teacher's reflection on-action, and shape curriculum design and implementation. For example, if a department's vision is to support learners in having meaningful experiences, that vision can support teachers in the department by providing a lens to choose the learning intentions/outcomes, activities, pedagogical approaches, and assessments that all align with the features of Meaningful PE.

Teacher reflection-in-action involves the professional judgements and decisions teachers make during the act of teaching itself (Schön, 1983). Whilst we have curriculum documents and lesson plans linked to learning objectives, we must also be responsive to the emerging events within our lessons. The *features* of Meaningful PE have provided me with a framework for both observation and intervention to enhance the children's attributed value to PE and the forms of movement they are taking part in. In this chapter I will explain how I use the features of Meaningful PE as an in-the-moment reflection tool, called the *Equalizer*, to guide my actions in lessons to ensure I attend to the creation of more meaningful experiences.

Scanning for cues to reduce the complexity of teaching PE

The learning objective of the lesson was to develop and refine the students' forward drive technique in cricket. I had provided the students with a model of what a good technical shot looks like and then demonstrated to them how to practice in pairs. Each mini practice session of 5–6 minutes was focused on one of four key elements: grip, stance, back lift, and follow through. Each key element was then further broken down into two or three technical points. As one partner was playing their shot from a stationary ball on a tee, the other was providing them feedback on one of the technical points from the key element being focused on (e.g., back lift). Prepare, hit the ball, receive feedback, and repeat. The key elements and technical points gave me an observation and intervention model. If I saw incorrect technique I would step in and offer corrective instruction. I was everywhere, interacting with everyone. 'Lift your bat higher,' 'Put your weight onto your front foot,' 'Hands together with a V-shaped grip,' 'Get your head straight,' 'Get your feet comfortably apart,' 'Don't bend your back,' 'Knees slightly bent.' This happened over the course of the entire lesson.

This vignette is an example of how I used to teach before coming across the Meaningful PE approach. Teaching 30 children in a PE lesson is a complex endeavour. We often deal with the deluge of information by reducing it to what we believe is important. In the vignette, my framework for observing and intervening was through a motor competence lens, specifically, if the individual was performing the movement incorrectly to the model I had supplied. This meant that much of my teaching involved scanning for cues about their hands, feet, head, and bat, and my intervention was predominantly corrective instruction (but could be similarly applied to most other PE content). This was a traditional framework for making sense of the information a busy PE lesson might offer us. An example of how I applied this type of traditional framework is provided in Table 5.1. We reduce the complexity of teaching by reducing what we are looking for and how we might intervene.

Table 5.1 A traditional framework for observing and intervening in physical education

Traditional framework		
Scanning	Potential cues	Action
Technique	Incorrect technique in comparison to model	Corrective instruction, feedback, and practice

The Equalizer

An issue of using a traditional framework such as that presented in Table 5.1 is that we can often focus on and get caught up in the minute details of the lesson whilst forgetting the bigger picture of our subject. This issue led me to ask myself: How does my constant corrective instruction on batting technique in cricket link to one of PE's grander espoused purposes of getting children to value and engage in a physically active lifestyle? I came to the conclusion that it may for some, but for many it may have the exact opposite impact to what we are hoping for.

In my search for a better framework linked to the bigger picture of the purposes of PE, I came across the *features* of Meaningful PE, which are presented as an evidence-based framework, that build on Kretchmar's (2000, 2006) work and represent the qualities of meaningful experiences in PE, youth sport, and physical activity. According to Beni, Fletcher, and Ní Chróinín (2017), a critical aspect of these features is that they are not a checklist to achieve but are integrated and influence each other.

A blog post on the LAMPE (2017) website presented the idea of a clock or watch mechanism to highlight this. In that metaphor, each feature works with another feature in promoting a meaningful experience, just like the cogs in a watch work with each other to move the hands. This was interesting but did not make much personal sense to me: I visualized the features as a sound equalizer (see Figure 5.1), a tool used to adjust the tones, volumes, and frequencies of musical signals. In thinking with an Equalizer, all the features are always present in our lessons but the teacher has the ability to either amplify or dampen them individually or collectively in pursuit of providing a more meaningful experience to the children we are teaching.

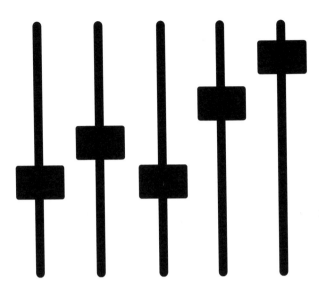

Figure 5.1 The Equalizer

When teaching, we need to tune in to what is happening and consider the meaningfulness of the experience, not just to the class but also the individual. This requires stepping back and observing from a distance, allowing us to see the bigger picture. Most times we are so focused on the teaching of techniques that we forget what the experience looks like as a whole. To use the Equalizer metaphor, in order to make our lessons more meaningful to the children we teach, they require us to strengthen or weaken one or a number of the features.

Searching for clues to absorb the complexity of teaching PE

The Equalizer adapts the *features* of Meaningful PE into a framework for professional judgement and decision-making. Rather than attempting to reduce the complexity of the information on offer through a prescriptive command and control approach that a traditional framework provides, the features of Meaningful PE encourage us to absorb that complexity into our teaching. If we reduce the information we look for and use, we are less likely to be flexible to what emerges in the lesson.

In shifting away from the traditional framework, scanning for prescribed cues is replaced by noticing potential clues that are linked to the *features* of Meaningful PE (see Table 5.2). This allowed me to move away from

Table 5.2 Observational clues framed by Meaningful PE

Meaningful experiences in PE		
Noticing	*Potential clues*	*Possible actions*
Motor competence	Harmful actions, incorrect actions, result of actions	A range of different responses depending on what events emerge out of the lesson
Social interaction	Positive communication when playing, negotiation when solving problems, asking questions	
Fun	Laughter, smiles, excitement	The clue noticed in one feature may require a response in an alternative feature
Challenge	Effort, engagement, success rate	
Personally relevant learning	Comments and feedback about activity, answers to questions	

planned, explicit responses that are formal, ordered, and often about the short-term improvement of performance, to flexible and adaptable responses through ongoing observation, dialogue, and negotiation for the long-term improvement of valuing of a physically active lifestyle through the provision of more meaningful experiences within PE.

In the following passages I provide three practical examples from my own teaching of how I have used the Equalizer metaphor. I am able to compare and contrast using both the traditional framework and the Equalizer as I have taught the same lessons and schemes of work over a period of a decade. In that time, I moved from scanning for cues to noticing clues. The examples demonstrate that by changing the framework, the information I deemed important also changed, which in turn led to a change of action. The changes of action are based on attending to the provision of a more meaningful experience to the children within my lessons.

Example 1: Grade 9 gymnastics – vaulting

This was a typical traditional vaulting lesson with a number of springboards, bucks, boxes, and lines of students waiting for their turn to jump.

Traditional framework

As shown in Table 5.3, all students would be doing the same vault, over the same height, at the same time. This allowed me to scan for technical deficiencies in their takeoff, flight, and landing, which allowed me to provide corrective feedback and instruction

Table 5.3 Traditional framework of observing vaulting

Traditional framework		
Scanning	*Cues*	*Actions*
Technique	Takeoff and landing mechanics	Corrective instruction and feedback

The Equalizer framework

As illustrated in Table 5.4, the Equalizer framework allowed me to notice how little *social interaction* was occurring, how there was more waiting to vault than actually vaulting, and that the level of *challenge* was optimal for very few students. This led to changes in my actions, which are noted in the right-hand column.

Table 5.4 The Equalizer framework for observing vaulting

Meaningful experiences in PE		
Noticing	*Potential clues*	*Actions*
Motor competence	Lots of lines and waiting, which results in not much practice	Introduced animal walks back from vaulting to develop strength and motor control
Social interaction	Very quiet; only spotters were talking	Groups had to design their own vaulting criteria, which they used to assess vaults and give peer feedback. This also supported personal relevance.
Challenge	All had to perform same vault over same height	Vaults of different heights and takeoff equipment were added and individuals could choose which to use and how to vault over them

Example 2: Grade 7 rugby – principles of rugby game play

The department I was leading had embraced a Game Sense approach. For Grade 7 students this meant that we designed lead-up or representative games linked to the principles of play of a particular game or sport. The examples in Tables 5.5 and 5.6 are from an introductory lesson of rugby, which looked at the principle of 'go forward'.

Traditional framework

The cue I was scanning for was poor decision-making about the attacking team going forward. Every time there was a mistake, I would stop the game, highlight the mistake, go through the correct decision, and ensure they could enact that decision before I allowed them to play again. This is shown in Table 5.5.

Table 5.5 Traditional framework of observing rugby game principles

Traditional framework		
Scanning	*Cues*	*Actions*
Decision-making	Observing an incorrect decision when the attacking team is going forward	Freeze game, highlight poor decision, and tell correct decision related to going forward

The Equalizer framework

I noticed very quickly that I was the dominant voice and was not allowing players to **interact** with each other and make their own decisions (**autonomy**). The changes this led to are shown in Table 5.6.

Table 5.6 The Equalizer framework for observing rugby game principles

Meaningful experiences in PE		
Noticing	*Potential clues*	*Action*
Social interaction	My voice dominated the lesson and I made the decisions for them	Support teams to formulate their own plans on how to 'go forward', implement, and review their success through guided questioning

Example 3: Grades 12 and 13 lacrosse – Transition

This was an optional curriculum activity that students could choose to prepare for playing against other schools. The focus of the lesson was movement off the ball and zonal positioning when transitioning from attack to defence.

Traditional framework

An external coach and I would scan players' movement off the ball when transitioning from attack to defence and observe how they set their zonal box defence. As shown in Table 5.7, when a poor decision was made or when we perceived a lack of effort, the team would run prescribed drills over and over again before they were put back into a game scenario.

Table 5.7 Traditional framework of observing transitioning in lacrosse

Traditional framework		
Scanning	Cues	Action
Movement off the ball	Lack of effort and poor decision-making	Run pre-planned drills as an intervention before putting back into a game scenario

The Equalizer framework

The framework allowed us to notice that the practice was not representative of a game situation; it gave far too much time for the defence to organize. We also noticed that we were organizing and prescribing the movement and strategies rather than allowing the players to be involved in the process. The changes made as a result of these observations are shown in Table 5.8.

Table 5.8 The Equalizer framework for observing transitioning in lacrosse

Meaningful experiences in PE		
Noticing	Potential clues	Action
Motor competence	Lack of transitions	Reduced pitch size so that transitions occurred more frequently
Social interaction	No communication between players in attack, defence, or transition	Organized learning teams to discuss how to solve the problem rather than leading whole squad talks
Challenge	Defence was always winning	Varied how teams lost possession so that the attacking team transitioning from defence had to self-organize

Moving forward with the Equalizer

Adopting the Equalizer has not been an easy process but it has been worthwhile. It made me question some long-held beliefs and practices I had about what good teaching in PE looks like. It also made me feel like a novice again, as breaking habits and building new ones is an uncomfortable process. I had to look for a more diverse range of informational clues and respond in a range of unplanned ways, mostly experimenting through trial and error. However, I did learn a few parameters along the way that can help someone who might wish to use the *features* of Meaningful PE as a framework for their in-the-moment judgement and decision-making:

1. Observation is more important than intervention

Our interactions have a significant impact on how meaningful an experience of PE is to a child. Counterintuitively, this starts by stepping back and observing. This requires both patience and an idea of what clues we are looking for related to *competence, social interaction, challenge, fun,* and *personally relevant learning*. We improve meaningful experiences for students by improving our actions as teachers, and we improve our actions through stepping back and observing.

2. Dialogue is an essential intervention

Whilst observation may provide us with some of the information required to improve our actions, it does not provide all of it. A key part of developing more meaningful experiences in PE is to start a dialogue with the children. If meaning is subjective, then dialogue is essential as it provides a chance for a child to explain something from their own perspective. This provides more information, especially about the feature of *personal relevance*, which generates more clues to act upon.

3. Do no harm with your interventions

Experiences in PE are on a spectrum, ranging from meaningful, useful, meaningless, and harmful. If attending to the creation of meaningful experiences becomes our primary method of observation and intervention, we must be acutely aware of any actions that have the potential of causing a child harm, not just physically but also psychologically and emotionally. There is an asymmetry at play within PE; that is, it may take hundreds of cumulative meaningful experiences to change sedentary behaviours to active ones, but only one harmful one to change active behaviours to sedentary.

4. The features are not a checklist

There will always be a temptation to take the features and develop them into some checklist. This is counter to its strength, that of a dynamic process that allows alternative solutions to emerge at the same time as problems are surfacing. A vital property of these features is that they are interrelated and interdependent on each other. For example, the clues that present as a *motor competence* issue that is preventing a more meaningful experience may require action in that feature but more than likely in one or a combination of the others, such as *challenge* or *personally relevant learning*.

Guiding principles of the Equalizer

To ensure that the framework does not turn into a prescriptive checklist but remains a search process that allows for open-ended perspectives and decision-making, I developed 'belief into action' statements related to Meaningful PE. The statements are underpinning assumptions that can assist in guiding teachers' actions for those who are committed to providing a more meaningful experience within PE and open them up to review, reflection, and refinement:

- We believe in *creating meaningful experiences* within PE . . . so we look to prioritize the interplay of fun, social interactions, challenge, motor competence, and personally relevant learning . . . and resist the urge to see them as by-products of participation.
- We believe that appropriate *challenge* leads to enjoyment and continued motivation . . . so we provide experiences that place an emphasis on the challenge inherent in the process of completing the task . . . and resist the urge to see challenge solely through the binary of winning and losing.
- We believe that developing *motor competence* is one of the best approaches to develop confidence . . . so we take a holistic approach to competence . . . and resist the urge to solve all physical problems with only physical solutions.
- We believe that *fun* is an essential part of creating meaningful experiences . . . so we seek to plan for fun by understanding our students' culture and community values . . . and resist the urge to prioritize fun at the expense of other meaningful criteria.
- We believe that positive *social interactions* are at the heart of meaningful movement experiences in PE . . . so we seek to carefully consider the way we organize opportunities for social interactions . . . and resist the urge to always control the relationships within the learning context.
- We believe that experiences in PE can be made more *personally relevant* . . . when we help co-create and connect the children's learning to their idea of a 'good life' beyond school . . . and resist the urge to assume what is important for us is important for them.

A personal reflection: connecting the dots to more meaningful experiences

Imagine each piece of information in a lesson is a single dot. In one lesson of PE there are hundreds of thousands of potential dots. The frame/s that we decide to use is vital to make sense of those dots. In the first place the frame/s act as a filter to decide what is even a dot. Next, they help us to decide which of those dots are important and which ones are irrelevant. The frame then allows us to figure how much detail we want about the dots we have decided are important. The sense-making only begins when we start connecting the important dots together (Klein, 2011).

Once we start connecting those dots, they help us to make sense of the events that have occurred and anticipate what might happen next. The frames we put around these dots have consequences for our actions and interactions. Defining what information is important shapes what we say and do in our lessons. By using the critical elements of meaningful experiences in PE, the Equalizer serves as a framework that helps in moving from scanning for cues in the misplaced hope of reducing the complexity of teaching to searching for clues. This, in turn, acknowledges and absorbs rather than reduces the complexity.

There is also a reciprocity at play regarding the frame we use in making sense of what is happening within our PE lessons. As we look to make sense of what is occurring within our lessons, we also become sense-givers. How we make sense of PE shapes the messages we convey to students about why movement and PE is important, what you may get from it, who can succeed, and how it might go about enriching their lives.

The Equalizer is a powerful framework to ensure we provide meaningful experiences of movement for children. If all significant adults in a child's life ensure as many movement experiences are as meaningful as possible, then we can begin to connect the dots at home, at school, and in youth sport and provide the best chance at producing people who use habitual daily movement as a way to flourish.

References

Beni, S., Fletcher, T., & Ní Chróinín, D. (2017). Meaningful experiences in physical education and youth sport: A review of the literature. *Quest, 69*, 291–312.

Klein, G. A. (2011). *Streetlights and shadows: Searching for the keys to adaptive decision making*. Cambridge, MA: MIT Press.

Kretchmar, R. S. (2000). Movement subcultures: Sites for meaning. *Journal of Physical Education, Recreation and Dance, 71*(5), 19–25.

Kretchmar, R. S. (2005). *Practical philosophy of sport and physical activity*. Champaign, IL: Human Kinetics.

Kretchmar, R. S. (2006). Ten more reasons for quality physical education. *Journal of Physical Education, Recreation and Dance*, *77*(9), 6–9.

LAMPE. (2017). *Using metaphors to think about the features of meaningful experiences*. Retrieved from https://meaningfulpe.wordpress.com/2017/09/28/using-metaphors-to-think-about-the-features-of-meaningful-experiences/.

Metheny, E. (1968). *Movement and meaning*. New York, NY: McGraw-Hill.

Schön, D. A. (1983). *The reflective practitioner: How professionals think in action*. New York, NY: Basic Books.

Tripp, D. H. (1993). *Critical incidents in teaching: The development of professional judgment*. London: Routledge.

Part III

Meaningful Physical Education by teacher educators

6 Meaningful PETE

Déirdre Ní Chróinín and Tim Fletcher

Introduction

In this chapter, we share our experiences of developing a pedagogical approach to physical education teacher education (PETE) to support pre-service teachers (PSTs) in Learning About Meaningful Physical Education (LAMPE). The chapter is divided into four sections: 1. How we initiated LAMPE, 2. Some challenges we encountered in developing LAMPE, 3. Five pedagogical principles that frame LAMPE, and 4. PST perspectives on LAMPE and Meaningful PE.

How we initiated LAMPE in our own teacher education practices

Common interests brought us together to initiate the Learning About Meaningful Physical Education (LAMPE) project in June 2013. Tim is a PE teacher educator with experience of PETE at both the high school and primary/elementary levels and is now based at Brock University, Canada. Déirdre is a PE teacher educator at the primary/elementary level for over fifteen years, based in Limerick, Ireland. We both had experience using self-study methodology to examine aspects of our pedagogical practice and a shared interest in improving our PETE practices. We were lucky that Professor Mary O'Sullivan agreed to mentor us in this project from the outset. Her expertise was invaluable in supporting us as we set out to develop an innovative pedagogical approach, particularly when we hit obstacles. She reassured us that there was value in the work we were doing around Meaningful PE, which helped us persevere and be successful in our efforts.

In this chapter, we share data generated across a four-year period during which we both committed to teaching with an eye towards teaching teachers about meaningful experiences. Initially, we drew on the writing of Blankenship and Ayers (2010), who advocated for and proposed pedagogies associated with joy-oriented PETE. These included an explicit emphasis on joy through language and the structure and organization of activities in PETE. Déirdre implemented these ideas in an introductory course on teaching PE for future generalist primary/elementary teachers in Ireland. Tim implemented the approach through developmental games courses for future PE teachers in Canada. Struggling together to articulate our focus and making sense of the literature on what joy-oriented approaches entailed led us, over time, to adopting 'meaningfulness' as an organizing concept that represented our shared understanding of what we were working toward.

Across the four-year period, we drew on a number of sources to support our developing ideas. For example, at the end of the first year we conducted an 'expert' member check (Braun & Clarke, 2013) with four PE scholars who had published papers on teaching for meaningful experiences and had helped us to develop our pedagogical approach. Their responses were directive in helping to distil and make the approach distinctive. We also shared our research at national and international conferences to get the perspectives of peers. Some of them pointed us in new directions and asked insightful questions that led us to make connections with other scholars in this area, such as Justen O'Connor. We published our findings at regular intervals to position our work within current physical education discourse and to receive feedback from reviewers of our work. We were particularly encouraged by the support of Mikael Quennerstedt who, in his Cagigal Scholar Lecture at the AIESEP World Congress in Edinburgh 2018, cited our work as one of several examples that offer 'hope for physical education' (Quennerstedt, 2019, p. 619). The development of LAMPE was not without its challenges, however, and we turn to these in the next section.

Challenges in developing LAMPE

In this section, we outline and analyze some of the challenges we faced in developing a pedagogical innovation focused on meaningful experiences and share how we addressed these challenges over several years.

Lack of empirical evidence

Starting out, there was little empirical evidence of what meaningfulness looked like in PE contexts, particularly from the teacher's point of view. For example, we were unsure about what pedagogies might facilitate meaningful experiences or how we could support PSTs to learn how to prioritize meaningfulness for learners. To begin addressing these gaps, we first sketched out what school-based Meaningful PE entailed and identified pedagogies that aligned with this conception. We turned to the work of PE scholars who have argued in conceptual or philosophical terms for the adoption of an approach that prioritizes meaningful participation in PE (Blankenship & Ayers, 2010; Kretchmar, 2000, 2001, 2006; Rintala, 2009) to guide our approach. Next, a commitment to promoting meaningful experience as a priority concept for school-based PE required understanding how teacher educators can support PSTs in learning how to do this in PETE programs. The writing of Metheny (1968) (in particular, the *Appendix for Educators*, p. 103–118), was useful in beginning to grapple with the role of *individual experience, language,* and *reflection* in meaningful experiences.

We also adopted Kretchmar's (2001, 2006) *features of meaningful experiences* as a framework to help direct our focus. Our adoption of these features was pragmatic as it provided us and our students (PSTs) with a shared point of departure that, in time, might allow for expansion of the framework and other representations of meaningful experiences. While we were concerned that these features might be read as reductive, narrowly constructed, or serve as a simple checklist, we were reassured that their value resided in how they have originated from the experiences of young learners (Beni, Fletcher, & Ní Chróinín, 2017). Across time, we and others (Lynch & Sargent, 2020; O'Connor, 2018; Walseth, Engebretsen, & Elvebakk, 2018), have begun to develop an evidence base related to the pedagogies of meaningful experiences in physical activity contexts.

Meaningfulness as individual and personal within a PE collective

Our positioning of meaningfulness as a personal interpretation caused some challenges in considering how to promote individual meaningfulness within a collective and highly social PE setting. Our major review of the literature (Beni et al., 2017) provided direction on some broad, common, qualitative elements of physical education experiences that were meaningful. At the same time, we sought out and embraced pedagogical strategies that facilitated how individuals could shape their own experiences, for example, through *teaching by invitation*. How teachers could access and respond to *student voice* has also been an important pedagogical approach that has helped us think about facilitating meaningful individual experiences and is one we have explored with the PSTs we teach. Again, with our students, we explored the potential gap between the aspirations of individualization with the reality of PE classes of more than 70 children. We resigned ourselves that teachers may not be in a position to adopt all aspects of Meaningful PE in their local contexts, and accepted that implementation 'by degree', based on what *was* possible in local contexts, could positively influence the practices of school PE.

Distinguishing the approach

At times, we were nervous about the novelty of our approach. Though we could see firsthand the value of focusing on meaningfulness in supporting our PSTs' learning in our own contexts, through discussion at academic conferences and reviews on journal article submissions we were met with questions such as: *Is this not just 'good' teaching? Does everyone not teach towards meaningful experiences?* These types of questions led us to rearticulate our theoretical and conceptual positioning. In response, we sought to identify ways LAMPE could be both similar to and distinct from generic descriptions of 'good teaching' that we and others shared with PSTs. We created space for PSTs to identify the key features of good teaching practice that were evident in Meaningful PE, but also made clear the distinctiveness of our approach, which was that we emphasized meaningfulness as the main *filter for all pedagogical decision-making*. Many of the PSTs we worked with embraced Meaningful PE as a valuable framework to guide their beginning experiences of teaching physical education. Most found the ideas of Meaningful PE and the features in particular as accessible (in terms of understanding and implementation) for them as beginning teachers. Next, we share how, across time, we identified elements of our practice that consistently supported Learning About Meaningful PE.

Pedagogical principles of LAMPE

Following a two-year collaborative process of planning, implementing, analyzing, reflecting, receiving feedback, modifying, and refining our pedagogies, we arrived at the point when we were ready to share LAMPE with confidence in its coherence and consistency. We drew on empirical data that provided evidence from both teacher educators' and PSTs' experiences to construct five pedagogical principles of LAMPE. Each pedagogical principle represents a variety of individual pedagogies and ideas for teacher educators that support PSTs who are learning to facilitate meaningful participation in school-based PE. These pedagogical principles, alongside supporting empirical data and sample pedagogies are outlined in detail elsewhere (Ní Chróinín, Fletcher, & O'Sullivan, 2018). In the following sections, we provide a brief outline of each of the principles.

Principle 1: Teacher educators explicitly prioritize meaningful participation in the planning, teaching, and assessment of PETE

The learning outcomes, design and delivery of content and learning activities, and assessment should have a clear and explicit relationship to learning about meaningfulness. Consistency across all aspects of teaching and learning reinforces a coherent message aligned with the ideas of meaningfulness.

Principle 2: Teacher educators model pedagogies that support meaningful experiences

Let PSTs see, hear, and feel pedagogies that facilitate meaningful experiences. Show PSTs a caring, interesting, and empathetic teacher by how you present yourself and relate to them as learners. Adopt *democratic approaches* that involve PSTs in decision-making and give them *choices* about what activity they engage in and with whom. Create spaces for PSTs to analyze their own experiences and your decision-making.

Principle 3: Support PSTs' engagement with features of meaningful participation as a learner and as a teacher

PSTs should be supported to engage in activities as a participant/learner and then to evaluate the meaningfulness of those experiences. *Reflection* on their own experiences as learners can help them to make sense of how to create similar experiences for others. PSTs also need opportunities to think in a teacher's role (for example, with a small group of children or peers) in order to test out pedagogies that facilitate meaningfulness. Evaluating these experiences provides further opportunities to consider how teachers gain insight on and make judgements about the quality of children's experiences in physical education.

Principle 4: Frame learning activities using features of meaningful participation

The *features of meaningful experiences in PE* (i.e., social interaction, fun, challenge, motor competence, personally relevant learning, and delight) (Beni et al., 2017) provide an accessible conceptual framework and language to support PSTs in planning for and analyzing PE experiences. Teacher educators need to be conscious not to limit PSTs' understanding of meaningful experiences to these features, but we suggest that the features have particular value with beginning teachers as a starting point to anchor their teaching practices that we would hope would expand and grow in time.

Principle 5: Support reflection on meaningfulness of PE experiences

Providing PSTs with longitudinal experiences of physical activity within PETE activity courses can be extremely challenging. *Reflection* on the meaningfulness of experiences by PSTs can relate to their own personal physical activity encounters and those of others, through digital and written cases, participant testimonies, and children's qualitative accounts of experience. A common language of meaningfulness is essential to enable PSTs to talk about and analyze their experiences, which is an important springboard to support them in scaffolding a *shared language* and understanding of meaningfulness with children in school-based PE.

These five pedagogical principles of LAMPE provided a foundation for our PETE practices. Importantly, adopting these pedagogical principles can support PSTs to embrace meaningfulness as the filter for their future PE practices. Next, we share some PSTs' experiences of LAMPE pedagogies and Meaningful PE.

PSTs' experiences of LAMPE (and Meaningful PE)

Across the four-year period that LAMPE was developed and enacted, we were regularly in contact with our PSTs in a variety of ways, such as collecting exit slips, informal conversations, and in-class discussions. Alongside these, as part of researching LAMPE, we collected data from PSTs about their experiences of LAMPE and Meaningful PE. We conducted 107 individual interviews, 14 focus group interviews with 35 participants, and collected 668 work samples and artefacts. Our overall finding (Fletcher, Ní Chróinín, O'Sullivan, & Beni, 2020) is that PSTs provide evidence of LAMPE supporting their learning about Meaningful PE, which indicates the value of teacher educators using the pedagogical principles of LAMPE as an anchor for PETE practice. Implementing pedagogies aligned with the five pedagogical principles of LAMPE helped PSTs learn (to varying degrees) why an emphasis on meaningful experiences is valuable to learners, what meaningful experiences entail, as well as how to implement pedagogies that prioritize the facilitation of Meaningful PE experiences. PSTs justified the promotion of meaningful experiences in schools by discussing its perceived value for learners and expressed a commitment to using practices that promoted Meaningful PE in their future practices. PSTs drew on the language of the features of meaningful experiences (Beni et al., 2017) to describe what meaningful experiences tend to consist of. PSTs outlined a priority on *student-centred and autonomy-supportive approaches*, and most could link specific strategies to particular *features* of meaningful experiences. Overall, PSTs' understanding of how meaningfulness could shape and direct their pedagogical decision-making varied. The consistent use of the professional language captured by LAMPE pedagogies and Meaningful PE (Beni et al., 2017) provides encouragement that meaningfulness is a priority in their approach to PE.

We believe that LAMPE offers a coherent and ***shared language*** that can be used across teacher education programs, while also being flexible enough to allow individual teacher educators and PSTs to emphasize certain features of Meaningful PE based on personal beliefs or, more importantly, the needs and interests of students in their local contexts. Also, by connecting and enabling the articulation of the why, what, and how of Meaningful PE, the shared language of LAMPE may provide one direction for reducing the theory-practice gap and for focusing the purposes of PETE. A number of PETE programs around the world now use ideas and approaches from LAMPE with PSTs. Our LAMPE team was honoured to be invited to deliver a keynote workshop to teacher educators from around the world at the first International Primary PE Seminar, July 25, 2018, that was organized by the European Primary Physical Education Network. The openly accessible resources available on the LAMPE website (https://meaningfulpe.wordpress.com) provide teacher educators with guidance on teaching toward meaningfulness, and we continue to seek ways to support the future expansion of LAMPE in new contexts.

References

Beni, S., Fletcher, T., & Ní Chróinín, D. (2017). Meaningful experiences in physical education and youth sport: A review of the literature. *Quest, 69*, 291–312.

Blankenship, B., & Ayers, S. F. (2010). The role of PETE in developing joy-oriented physical educators. *Quest, 62*, 171–183.

Braun, V., & Clarke, V. (2013). *Successful qualitative research.* London: Sage.

Fletcher, T., Ní Chróinín, D., O'Sullivan, M., & Beni, S. (2020). Pre-service teachers articulating their learning about meaningful physical education. *European Physical Education Review, 26*, 885–902.

Kretchmar, R. S. (2000). Movement subcultures: Sites for meaning. *Journal of Physical Education, Recreation and Dance, 71*(5), 19–25.

Kretchmar, R. S. (2001). Duty, habit, and meaning: Different faces of adherence. *Quest, 53*, 318–325.

Kretchmar, R. S. (2006). Ten more reasons for quality physical education. *Journal of Physical Education, Recreation and Dance, 77*(9), 6–9.

Lynch, S., & Sargent, J. (2020). Using the meaningful physical education features as a lens to view student experiences of democratic pedagogy in higher education. *Physical Education and Sport Pedagogy*, 1–14.

Metheny, E. (1968). *Movement and meaning.* New York, NY: McGraw-Hill.

Ní Chróinín, D., Fletcher, T., & O'Sullivan, M. (2018). Pedagogical principles of learning to teach meaningful physical education. *Physical Education and Sport Pedagogy, 23*, 117–133.

O'Connor, J. (2019). Exploring a pedagogy for meaning-making in physical education. *European Physical Education Review, 25*, 1093–1109.

Quennerstedt, M. (2019). Physical education and the art of teaching: Transformative learning and teaching in physical education and sports pedagogy. *Sport, Education and Society, 24*, 611–623.

Rintala, J. (2009). It's all about the -ing. *Quest, 61*, 278–288.

Walseth, K., Engebretsen, B., & Elvebakk, L. (2018). Meaningful experiences in PE for all students: An activist research approach. *Physical Education and Sport Pedagogy, 23*, 235–249.

7 Learning to teach generalist primary teachers how to prioritize meaningful experiences in physical education

Maura Coulter, Richard Bowles and Tony Sweeney

Introduction

In this chapter, we discuss our experiences as three teacher educators who have used Learning About Meaningful Physical Education (LAMPE) as we have worked with pre-service generalist primary school teachers (PSTs) in three separate universities in Ireland. Together, we have a wide range of experience delivering primary physical education teacher education (PETE). We are also experienced coaches, having worked with young children right through to elite adults in a variety of sports. Our own sporting experiences include international rugby, county Gaelic football, athletics, golf, hiking, and geocaching. In our PETE practices, we draw on a range of curriculum models and approaches, such as game sense and positive coaching, and position ourselves as lifelong learners, continually adapting and updating our approaches.

We were drawn to the ideas of LAMPE partly because they resonated with our personal philosophies, and we anticipated they might provide a useful and accessible framework for PSTs who were learning to teach PE. Maura and Richard had previously participated in the international LAMPE project (Bowles, Fletcher, Coulter, Gleddie, & Ni Chroinin, 2019). During that time we had come to understand the *features* of Meaningful PE (the 'what') (Beni, Fletcher, & Ní Chróinín, 2017) in our first year of introducing LAMPE; however, we felt we needed to explore ways to improve our practices as teacher educators by further utilizing the *pedagogical principles* of LAMPE (the 'how') (Ní Chróinín, Fletcher, & O'Sullivan, 2018). Tony became interested in LAMPE through attendance at various conferences and subsequent engagement with the literature. The three of us agreed to work together the following academic year with the intention of learning more about LAMPE and exploring how we might embed the pedagogical principles of LAMPE in our own contexts. In this chapter, we describe how we used LAMPE in one semester with three cohorts of PSTs in their third and fourth years of study within a primary teacher education program.

In Ireland, generalist primary teachers deliver all curriculum areas. PSTs are therefore required to complete modules in curriculum and pedagogies for 11 different subject areas. One of the three cohorts we taught and studied was a third-year group in a required PETE module. The other two cohorts had already completed core modules and were now participating in an elective or specialism module. This suggests these PSTs had a particular interest in PE. Content of the modules included Outdoor and Adventure Activities, Games, and Adapted Physical Education. In their programs to date, PSTs had engaged with concepts including curricular integration, assessment for learning, and differentiation. They had also gained insights into other foundation areas such as human development, philosophy and psychology, which informed their understanding of the child-centred focus that is central to the Irish Primary School Curriculum. All PSTs had completed school placements during the first two years of their program. These experiences positioned PSTs to critically engage with analysis of, and reflection on, pedagogy in PE.

To illustrate our experiences, we use extracts from conversations and written reflections we shared with each other, teaching resources, and feedback from PSTs. We share how our *collaborative planning, shared experiences,* and *reflective practice* helped to shape and support our implementation of LAMPE. We outline how we used resources from the LAMPE website (https://meaningfulpe.wordpress.com) and broad ideas about Meaningful PE to scaffold discussion and encourage PST engagement with academic literature. We also share how we explored a range of curricular content utilizing LAMPE (e.g., outdoor and adventure activities, games, adapted physical education) with PSTs. Finally, we discuss possibilities for teacher educators as they embark on learning about using LAMPE in their teacher education programs.

Collaboration for learning

> This is the importance of the reflection, post-reflection, and the support –
> the internal kind of critical friendship – that gives to each of us as teacher
> educators to actually be able to talk about these things and to try and tease
> them out.
>
> Richard

There has been an increasing trend for PE teacher educators to examine their own practice, with a view to supporting their professional learning.

As we began exploring LAMPE it was very beneficial to learn from and be supported by colleagues familiar with the approach through being part of an international community of practice. We felt secure we were undertaking a learning journey where we could share our thoughts, concerns, and uncertainties with others. We built on the work of Goodyear and Casey (2015) who advocate 'for inter-professional collaboration with researcher(s) who cross the boundary of their institutions . . . to facilitate change' (p. 201). We found that this type of collaboration guided and supported our exploration of LAMPE and was a useful framework through which to examine our own learning through *reflection* and critical friendship.

Our initial objective was to describe how we would introduce the *features* of Meaningful PE (Beni et al., 2017) to PSTs in the modules we were teaching and establish how we could frame learning activities for PSTs within our individual contexts. The next objective was to examine our pedagogies of teacher education in order to develop a fuller understanding of the pedagogical principles of LAMPE to foster PSTs' engagement. The sharing of reflections, feedback, and dialogue impacted positively on the short-term planning and teaching of subsequent lessons.

Developing pedagogies of teacher education

> Connecting our students' experiences to 'real life' situations is very important in order to stimulate debate and critical thinking. The pedagogical cases [from the LAMPE website] are a good way of doing this. By making PE 'meaningful' for our students we may be prompting them to facilitate meaningful experiences for their own pupils.
>
> Richard

The growing range of literature and online resources focusing on LAMPE (for teacher educators) and the Meaningful PE approach (for school teachers) had a twofold effect on our teaching. Firstly, several articles and blog posts helped guide our planning and discussion as we considered the pedagogical principles of LAMPE that support PSTs' learning. These principles involved explicit prioritization of meaningful participation; modelling and exploration of pedagogies for meaningful experiences; PSTs engaging as learners, participants, and teachers; framing activities using the features of meaningful experiences; and supporting PSTs to reflect on the meaningfulness of PE (Ní Chróinín et al., 2018).

Secondly, the work of Beni, Ní Chróinín, and Fletcher (2019), and Ní Chróinín, Beni, Fletcher, Griffin, and Price (2019) provided us with academic literature to guide discussion and *reflection* with PSTs. We used group discussions in class to prompt PSTs to consider their own understanding and that of their peers in relation to meaningful experiences in PE. For example, Tony's use of an online discussion forum prompted PSTs to ask and answer one another's questions in response to these readings. The experiences of the teachers who implemented preliminary ideas about Meaningful PE in these particular articles were identified by both PSTs and us as useful and valuable. In particular, the decision-making required by newly qualified generalist teachers (e.g., Beni et al., 2019) resonated strongly with them. As a result, the readings helped frame in-class discussions, and the PSTs began to share their own experiences more fully. One of our students said:

> I think it was the teacher, Stephanie [in Beni et al., 2019], looking at her reflections, and how she tried to plan for the different [features] of Meaningful PE separately, but then she realized you can't really do that. [It] was helpful to know how she thought or how she planned for it. So, when you go out, you can nearly look at the way she did it and think about how you do it. I just thought it was good to see it from another teacher's perspective.

To support our teacher education practice, we also utilized pedagogical cases published on the LAMPE website. These cases acted as a stimulus for our own discussions initially and subsequently with PSTs in class. For example, we used the 'cogs of a clock' and 'Equalizer' metaphors (Pedagogical Case #4 on the LAMPE website and Chapter 5 in this volume, respectively) to help us think about trying not to include all features in a lesson but rather focusing on specific features at appropriate times. Another student considered this approach:

> I thought looking at those case studies . . . showed how Meaningful PE works. There were [features] in each one of them. I remember the running one. Like how you basically made a pretty boring PE activity into one that was meaningful by giving social interaction, challenge, all those elements. Yeah, so I thought looking at those [cases] was really helpful.

In utilizing LAMPE for an Outdoor and Adventure Activities module, Maura emphasized the features of *fun* and *social interaction* when undertaking team challenges and, later, *delight* when the tasks were completed successfully. As we used these metaphors to support how we thought about the features, we supported PSTs to develop their understanding that meaningful experiences for students could be an outcome of good planning and teaching. PSTs noted how some ideas about Meaningful PE were evident in curriculum models that we had been including in our teaching. For example, the PSTs undertaking the Outdoor and Adventure module saw an alignment between Meaningful PE and elements of the Adventure Education and Outdoor Education curriculum models. In particular, they noted how concepts such as providing *challenge* (Tannehill & Dillon, 2007) and being *child-centred* (Williams & Wainwright, 2016) resonated with their exploration of Meaningful PE. In addition, discussions on acknowledging *the child's voice* and supporting the development of the learners' *autonomy* provided opportunities to talk about *personally relevant learning*. The pedagogical approach underpinning this process highlighted the co-construction of knowledge between teachers and children, the potential for experiential learning, and the importance of regular 'reviewing . . . to support transfer of learning' (Williams & Wainwright, 2016, p. 590).

Following a scavenger hunt activity, PSTs completed a chart (Figure 7.1) where they placed a Post-It Note along a continuum to identify how meaningful they found the activity. In this example, it is clear that the PSTs found *motor competence* to contribute less to the meaningfulness in this activity compared to *fun* and *personally relevant learning*.

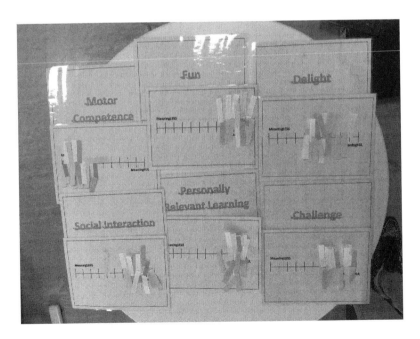

Figure 7.1 PSTs' Meaningful PE continuum chart

Discussions with PSTs at the end of each class allowed us to reflect on the meaningfulness they experienced. One PST commented:

> I thought that the continuum charts that you did with us, where you use the Post-It Notes to mark it off on each feature, were really good. I thought that was great. I'd definitely use that in the future as well, I think.

This led to further reflection on how they might create similar experiences in their future classrooms. In this way, we were able to blend theory and practice, exploring 'concrete examples of what things looks like' (Lawrence, 2018, p. 129). We became more effective at including the pedagogical principles of LAMPE into our teaching and continued to reflect and check in to establish if PSTs not only understood the 'what' but also the 'how' of Meaningful PE. Therefore, while engaging with the pedagogical principles of LAMPE as teacher educators, we were also engaging with Meaningful PE as an approach for PSTs as future teachers at the same time. The PSTs concluded that, as teachers, the features of Meaningful PE would be much easier to implement in their own classrooms in the future (rather than on school placement) as they would know the children, their backgrounds, and the school context better and therefore, they could plan much more effectively.

Our experiences suggest teacher educators should ***model pedagogies*** that support meaningful experiences so that PSTs have the opportunity to experience these approaches practically. This may include the teacher educator being intentional and explicit in using strategies that support ***autonomy*** (e.g., enabling PSTs to use voice and choice in their learning) and providing experiences that support the development of, for example, ***motor competence***. Moreover, we believe that teacher educators articulating the reasons for their pedagogical decisions regarding LAMPE will encourage PSTs to critically evaluate such choices in their own future practice. The resulting discussion could involve PSTs unpacking and critiquing the teacher educators' reasons for their practice, thereby creating opportunities for pedagogical inquiry. For example, following a practical class on inclusive strategies for students with special needs, PSTs were asked to consider the meaningfulness of their experience. One PST reflected on the level of challenge they had experienced:

> Children's motivation can also be fostered by incorporating an element of challenge into PE, as providing children with appropriately challenging tasks resulting in success will encourage the children to be proud of their performance, leading to more interest and a willingness to take on more challenging activities.

In our teaching, LAMPE and Meaningful PE were used to support the development of a **shared language** through creating a coherent platform for teacher educators and PSTs to articulate their professional knowledge by reimagining (why) and recreating (what and how) the practices of Meaningful PE to better address the needs of learners.

Reflections on content and pedagogy

Why are we so content-focused? I'm improving at facilitating these discussions and giving the students voice but at the loss of content, and this is the dilemma. I'm finding the reflection so worthwhile and necessary, and if we want students to do it with children, we should surely model it. But I am battling with losing content!

Maura

Although we found it challenging, we suggest teacher educators should aim to position PSTs simultaneously as learners who are engaging in and experiencing meaningful forms of PE, and learners who are learning about teaching in ways that prioritize meaningfulness in PE (i.e., developing pedagogical skills). Tasks, activities, and experiences should be designed, selected, and reflected upon based on their potential to support engagement with the features of Meaningful PE and underpinned by pedagogies that support meaningful experiences. Therefore, PSTs can be provided with opportunities to reflect on the meaningfulness of their own school and university PE experiences and how these experiences might inform their future practice. PSTs were quick to appreciate the value of this to allow them '*as teachers, to reflect on whether a change in our practice must be brought about for the benefit of the pupils and to continue the stream of Meaningful PE experience*'. They also recognized the impact for their students' learning: '*because sometimes the kids don't actually realize what they've learned until they actually think about it themselves*'.

In terms of our learning about LAMPE, we first used the **features** of Meaningful PE (Beni et al., 2017) to frame and reflect on our learning as teacher educators. Then, by reflecting on the content at the end of each of our lessons, we examined where features were evident or where they might have been made more explicit in class. We did this by making time for a 'check-in' discussion with PSTs as part of our lesson conclusion. This occurred through looking at how meaningful PSTs' learning was and by reflecting on the pedagogical approaches they experienced as learners. Figure 7.2 shows how a class of PSTs reflected on experiencing **motor competence** using a visual method.

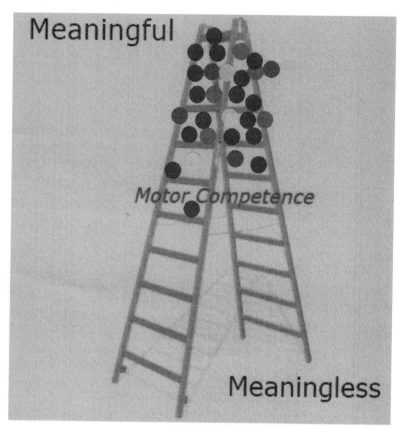

Figure 7.2 An end-of-class response to motor competence as part of a meaningful
     experience

Many PSTs commented that this **reflection** time aligned with 'good teaching'
practices in other curricular areas, and the features were accessible and easy to
understand. It was interesting too that as the PSTs were learning to become
generalist teachers, they saw parallels and recognized the value of teaching for
meaningful learning across other subjects. As one PST said: '*I think you can
apply those meaningful components to most subjects, really*'. LAMPE brought
a focus to the value of learning in PE for another PST who stated:

> It is crucial to show the children that what we learn in PE is just as
> important as what we learn in maths, and the skills acquired can be
> incorporated and transferred to many other subjects or areas of life.

As illustrated in Figures 7.1 and 7.2, initially we used the terms 'meaningful' and 'meaningless' as descriptors. Following our discussions and reading of Beni et al. (2019), we now suggest that the phrase 'less meaningful' rather than 'meaningless' should be used at one end of a continuum of meaning because it better reflects the responses of our PSTs.

From an administrative perspective, using LAMPE within our modules presented each of us with challenges. For example, we are required to submit our module outlines to our university program boards for approval up to 18 months in advance of an academic year. Therefore, when we initiated our exploration of LAMPE we were trying to embed it into previously approved modules. Our discussions highlighted the pressure to deliver approved module content while exploring the features and pedagogical principles of LAMPE. Much of the approach would have been evident in our teaching prior to explicit engagement with LAMPE but we agreed that the practice of 'checking in' with PSTs as a *reflective process* needed to be prioritized regardless of the potential loss of module content as a result.

When we embarked on using and exploring LAMPE, an important consideration for each of us was how to incorporate authentic discussion into our classes while at the same time covering a sufficient range of content to enable our PSTs to teach effectively. We were particularly conscious that our time with PSTs was limited and we were concerned that we might be neglecting some areas of curriculum content. As the lack of PE contact time with generalist PSTs is well documented internationally (Tsangaridou & Kyriakides, 2018), we did not wish to further disadvantage our own students. Our experiences using the pedagogical principles of LAMPE, however, have been very positive. We now believe that opportunities for 'checking in' enhanced our teaching and helped our students to develop a deeper understanding of teaching of PE in primary schools. Consequently, we suggest that generalist primary physical education teacher educators exploring LAMPE for the first time engage with the features as a starting point before progressing to the pedagogical principles (Ní Chróinín et al., 2018) due to the role that the *features* play in several of the pedagogical principles themselves.

Concluding thoughts

> There is a productive association now from my students that looking at Meaningful PE will support the provision of quality PE teaching and learning . . . [leading] toward a consideration of what this will look like in terms of pedagogy and practice.
>
> Tony

When we started exploring LAMPE, we were unsure whether it was a philosophy, a curriculum model, a teaching strategy, or a combination of all three. We have come to believe that LAMPE is an overarching approach that can be used in conjunction with curriculum models or as an independent approach for teacher educators. Within our modules, we were exploring a variety of curriculum models, including Teaching Personal and Social Responsibility, Adventure Education, Teaching Games for Understanding, and Co-operative Learning. We found that it was possible to embed teaching for meaningfulness while providing our students with meaningful learning opportunities within each model.

Our experiences illustrate how the pedagogical principles of LAMPE provided a guiding framework that influenced our ***pedagogical decision-making*** and actions in our teacher education practice within individual learning activities as well as within module content, design, and organization. We found LAMPE to be valuable in supporting PSTs' learning and helped illustrate to PSTs the value of teaching from a coherent set of principles focused on meaningful learning experiences. This process helped to inform PSTs' own decision-making about their actions and children's learning, and they found the language very accessible.

In terms of our process of engaging with LAMPE, the value of a community of practice 'emphasizes the contribution of relationship, caring, and mutual support within the group while at the same time focusing on the professional development of individuals within their own discipline' (Brody & Hadar, 2015, p. 247). At the outset, we were concerned that our collaboration might be less productive because of the disparate module content that we were presenting in three different contexts. As we progressed, however, our reflections and discussions showed a consensus that LAMPE was an effective approach for each of us regardless of content and context. During our reflections we interrogated the quality of PSTs' experiences, whereby participation in PE is viewed as enriching lives (Kretchmar, 2006). Significantly, it provided us with opportunities to share and discuss ideas that contributed to our own professional learning as teacher educators. Our experiences highlight the importance of building on PSTs' previous experience as they learn to teach using the features of Meaningful PE and pedagogies that support meaningful experiences. We recognized the centrality of teacher educators' and PSTs' ***reflection*** as part of this learning process. In turn, we hope this can ultimately underline for PSTs the importance of teacher and student reflection within the primary school.

Exploring LAMPE collaboratively provided us with a lens through which to interrogate our practice. Working with other teacher educators reinforced our resolve and sustained us through adapting our practice, providing us with the necessary support and encouragement through sharing experiences, content, resources, and outcomes. Trying something new invigorated our teaching and made lessons more rewarding for us in return.

We each faced challenges as teacher educators when learning about and using LAMPE. We each wanted our own teaching to be meaningful for PSTs, so that their experiences might prompt them to plan and teach for meaningfulness in their classes in the future. We found the provision of the pedagogical case studies on the LAMPE website and relatable research articles to be useful and help our PSTs to engage with ideas about how to make PE meaningful for students. What we have learned in teaching PSTs through using LAMPE is that it is not just a hierarchical teacher educator-PST or teacher-child approach, but rather a more ***democratic*** '*we approach*', where everyone in the class is involved in ensuring that learning is meaningful, and that, for us, is what matters.

References

Beni, S., Fletcher, T., & Ní Chróinín, D. (2017). Meaningful experiences in physical education and youth sport: A review of the literature. *Quest, 69*, 291–312.

Beni, S., Ní Chróinín, D., & Fletcher, T. (2019). A focus on the how of meaningful physical education in primary schools. *Sport, Education and Society, 24*, 624–637.

Bowles, R., Fletcher, T., Coulter, M., Gleddie, D., & Ni Chroinin, D. (2019, April 7). *Using S-STEP to examine enactment of a pedagogical innovation in an international community of practice.* Presentation at the American Educational Research Association Annual Meeting, Toronto.

Brody, D. L., & Hadar, L. L. (2015). Personal professional trajectories of novice and experienced teacher educators in a professional development community. *Teacher Development, 19*, 246–266.

Goodyear, V., & Casey, A. (2015). Innovation with change: Developing a community of practice to help teachers move beyond the 'honeymoon' of pedagogical renovation. *Physical Education and Sport Pedagogy, 20*, 186–203.

Kretchmar, R. S. (2006). Ten more reasons for quality physical education. *Journal of Physical Education, Recreation and Dance, 77*(9), 6–9.

Lawrence, J. (2018). Teacher educators in primary physical education. In G. Griggs & K. Petrie (Eds.), *Routledge handbook of primary physical education* (pp. 122–133). Abingdon, UK: Routledge.

Ní Chróinín, D., Beni, S., Fletcher, T., Griffin, C., & Price, C. (2019). Using meaningful experiences as a vision for physical education teaching and teacher education practice. *Physical Education and Sport Pedagogy, 24*, 598–614.

Ní Chróinín, D., Fletcher, T., & O'Sullivan, M. (2018). Pedagogical principles of learning to teach meaningful physical education. *Physical Education and Sport Pedagogy, 23*, 117–133.

Tannehill, D., & Dillon, M. (2007). *A handbook of ideas: Teaching adventure education.* University of Limerick.

Tsangaridou, N., & Kyriakides, L. (2018). Pre-service primary physical educa-
    tion. In G. Griggs & K. Petrie (Eds.), *Handbook of primary physical education*
    (pp. 98–111). Abingdon, UK: Routledge.
Williams, A., & Wainwright, N. (2016). A new pedagogical model for adventure
    in the curriculum: Part two – outlining the model. *Physical Education and Sport
    Pedagogy, 21,* 589–602.

8 Teaching teachers about Meaningful Physical Education in a northern Canadian setting

Douglas Gleddie and Jodi Harding-Kuriger

Meaningful PE and our teaching philosophies

Doug is a professor in the Faculty of Education at the University of Alberta (UAlberta) and has been a teacher educator since 2008. His prior experiences include nine years of teaching in K-12 settings (a wide variety of subjects with a focus on PE) and six years as the Director of Ever Active Schools, which is a healthy schools organization that provides professional development and leadership in Alberta and across Canada for health and PE. Jodi is a PhD candidate at the UAlberta researching Meaningful PE. She is also a teacher educator working with pre-service teachers (PSTs) in primary/elementary PE. Jodi is an award-winning educator (for her work at the University and in schools) and has been an influential leader through the *Health and Physical Education Council* in Alberta as well as at the National level. Most importantly, she has taught PE for over 15 years in a number of different contexts and grades and is a reflective and thoughtful practitioner.

Our teaching philosophies draw heavily on John Dewey's theory of experience and education and inform the design and delivery of our classes. Taken together, our philosophies are based on the following premises:

> [T]he central problem of an education based upon experience is to select the kind of present experiences that live fruitfully and creatively in subsequent experiences.
>
> (Dewey, 1938, pp. 27–28)

Experience and education cannot be directly equated to each other. For some experiences are mis-educative. Any experience is mis-educative that has the effect of arresting or distorting the growth of further experience. An experience may be such as to engender callousness; it may produce lack of sensitivity and of responsiveness. Then the possibilities of having richer experience in the future are restricted.

(Dewey, 1938, pp. 25–26)

We also draw on professional development literature (for what is teacher education other than the development of professionals?) and further rely on a Deweyan conceptualization of continuous professional development (Armour, Quennerstedt, Chambers, & Makopoulo, 2017) that frames our teaching vision and practices. Armour et al. (2017) propose the following four goals for continuous professional development, each of which is expanded upon later in the chapter:

1   Acknowledge complex learning processes
2   Prioritize context and challenge
3   Praxis-focused
4   Nurture career-long growth

Over our careers we have also developed a fundamental belief in the critical, life-giving need for humans to move and to do so joyfully. That belief also informs our philosophies and guides our practices, providing another crucial part of the foundation in how we choose to support PSTs in their journeys toward becoming teachers of PE.

Our philosophies of teaching are rooted in our own experiences as K-12 teachers and as teacher educators. These experiences have enabled us to grow and develop as teachers and teacher educators, refine management and assessment skills, gain valuable insight into the social and cultural influences affecting students, families and communities, and have helped to define our personal and professional identities. We can see the threads of joyful, essential movement being woven into the fabric of who we are and what we feel PE should be. Those threads also form the basis of our relationships with PSTs and encourage us to meet them where they are.

With these premises in mind, the key connection to Meaningful PE in our respective philosophies is that of joyful movement (*delight*). As Kretchmar (2008) writes:

When movement is experienced as joy, it adorns our lives, makes our days go better, and gives us something to look forward to. When movement is joyful and meaningful, it may even inspire us to do things we never thought possible.

(p. 162)

We believe that students (both in schools and in universities) are often motivated by joy and work/play extremely hard to find it. As a bonus, they will also get health, social, and academic benefits among others.

Context

The Faculty of Education at UAlberta is based in Edmonton, which is the northernmost metropolitan area in Canada. UAlberta has one of the largest teacher education programs in the country. Our department focuses on preparing primary/elementary generalists (or classroom teachers) who will enter the field and be expected to teach eight distinct subject areas, including PE, in grades K-6. We are responsible for teaching the course: *Introduction to Curriculum and Pedagogy for Elementary Physical Education*. As part of our university's commitment to northern and Indigenous education, there are two unique, community-focused ways to earn a Bachelor of Education degree: (1) the Aboriginal Teacher Education Program (ATEP) (University of Alberta, 2020a) and (2) the Collaborative Program (University of Alberta, 2020b). The course we teach is offered to students in both programs.

The ATEP involves a longstanding partnership between our university and several smaller, rural academic institutions and communities across northern Alberta. The ultimate focus of the program is to 'improve the educational success of Aboriginal children' (University of Alberta, 2020a). As such, the program seeks to develop in PSTs a greater understanding of Aboriginal culture while integrating contemporary perspectives on teaching and learning. Key aspects of the program include developing teachers 'in community' and increasing the number of Aboriginal teachers in Alberta. Jodi has taught the primary/elementary PE course in the ATEP program at Northern Lakes College in the town of Slave Lake, and Doug has taught the course at Portage College (in Lac La Biche) and Maskwacis Cultural College (on the Maskwacis Reserve south of Edmonton). PSTs in ATEP tend to be older than those we teach in Edmonton. They also tend to have had a wider variety of life experiences, are often parents, and are usually approaching teaching as a second or third career.

The Collaborative Program is offered at a number of smaller colleges in rural and northern areas of Alberta. What this means is that PSTs in remote areas can get a UAlberta degree without having to leave their community. Doug has taught the primary/elementary PE course at Keyano College in Fort McMurray twice in the past three years. Similar to ATEP, the PSTs in the collaborative teacher education programs are older than those we teach at UAlberta, which means they often have more life experience. Teaching is often a second career choice made later in life and as a result, the classes have a mature feel to them. Students usually take strong ownership of their learning and are committed to becoming successful teachers and leaders in their community.

Meaningful PE guiding our practice: Why?

As explained previously, we see one of the main purposes of being a PE teacher or teacher educator as providing contexts for joyful or delightful movement. So how can we 'look for' this in our practice? Kretchmar (2008) posits:

> Children are built to move; they want to move. Almost anything can be turned into a grand adventure – catching, throwing, running, touching, enjoying rhythmic activities, and discovering 'fundamental movement concepts'. A teacher who has a gift for make-believe can, without much difficulty, become something of a Pied Piper of movement. Delight, excitement, intrigue, and usually considerable noise permeate the physical education setting.
>
> (p. 166)

We embed this ethos in our practice by drawing on a vision of Meaningful PE to guide our decision-making (Ní Chróinín, Beni, Fletcher, Griffin, & Price, 2019). Making the time to outline a vision for teaching encourages teacher educators and PSTs to consider their whole being as they approach teaching. A vision helps teachers or teacher educators articulate their thoughts about theoretical and practical knowledge. They can consider their affective side: their dreams, passions, and hopes for physical education. A vision also encourages consideration of the delivery of Meaningful PE – space, time, equipment, context, and the teacher's or teacher educator's own personal confidence and competence. Lastly, a vision honours the individual's spiritual knowledge about education (Wilson, 1995). Taking the time to consider education from and for the whole person may contribute to the evolution of visions of Meaningful PE (Ní Chróinín et al., 2019). This vision for teaching Meaningful PE is likely to evolve over time as teachers and/or teacher educators gain more experience in educational settings. 'However, having this vision alone does not result in changes to practice unless teachers encounter the right set of circumstances, such as context, support, [autonomy] and motivation, to implement this new vision' (Ní Chróinín et al., 2019, p. 600).

We call our vision 'bringing the skatepark to the gym'. A skatepark (where people go to skateboard) offers an environment in which people can play, be creative, make their own decisions, and choose their own challenges. If you go and observe a skatepark, you'll see people finding joy in learning, demonstrating intrinsic motivation, and constructing personal meaning – all without a trophy in sight. This type of environment requires movement to be honoured, not just used (Kretchmar, 2000). We want to move past a utilitarian or functional approach to movement (which does have its place) and help PSTs appreciate and experience learning through movement as potential sources of joy, delight, and meaningfulness. According to Kretchmar (2005, pp. 206–207), there are some ways we can move toward joy, delight, and meaningfulness, by shifting:

• From mechanically correct to expressive movement
• From effective to inventive to creative movement
• From movement as obligation to movement as part of your own story
• From fear and avoidance to accepting and overcoming a challenge
• From thinking to spontaneity

We believe that teacher educators can encourage these types of shifts by providing a rich learning environment for all students – both K-12 and PSTs alike – to play in, creating a culture of honoured movement, reflecting on our own practice and, perhaps most importantly, having our PSTs reflect on their practice and journeys of joyful movement. We ask PSTs to look for the following as they teach:

• Sweaty, smiling faces
• Grim-faced determination followed by quiet satisfaction
• Engaged and lively conversations between students
• Focus – the 'tongue out of the side of the mouth' kind
• Failure, then some more failure followed by overcoming a realistic challenge

If they can see the sorts of external signs we have shared in this list, we believe that the more internal and elusive aspects of joy may follow.

Meaningful PE guiding our practice: How?

> I looked forward to coming to class every day because [Doug] made learning meaningful and enjoyable. He made everyone feel welcome, confident, and capable. . . . I am leaving both courses with so much more knowledge and experience on how to make PE and Health enjoyable for my future students.
> Anonymous Student Feedback Form

As shown in this student comment, we try to create a safe and supportive environment for our PSTs to learn, fail, grow, connect, and succeed. Throughout this chapter, we offer several examples of tasks and assignments we use in our classes to highlight how several of the pedagogical principles of Learning About Meaningful PE (LAMPE) (Ní Chróinín, Fletcher, & O'Sullivan, 2018) are incorporated into our practices, including explicitly prioritizing meaningful participation, modelling pedagogies that support Meaningful PE, supporting engagement with the features, framing learning activities using the features, and supporting reflection.

In trying to foster a safe and supportive environment for PSTs, we explicitly prioritize meaningful participation and model pedagogies that support Meaningful PE by having the feature of *social interaction* occupy a central place in our teacher education practice. At the beginning of the course, as PSTs are getting to know us and one another, we purposefully take time to make social connections through small games and invitational activities. As we move further into the course and become more comfortable with one another, we take steps to allow several of the other features of meaningful experiences to emerge organically from PST experience (both prior to class and in class), as will be detailed in the following sections. Finally, we also explicitly bring the features of Meaningful PE to the forefront in class activities, discussions, and assessment.

Autobiographical assignment

The first assignment in the class is an autobiographical inquiry (Gleddie et al., 2017, p. 22) that is designed to have PSTs reflect on, inquire into, and share their educative and mis-educative experiences with PE and physical activity (recreation, sport, etc.). Not only does the assignment encourage PSTs to examine their own relationship to movement and the ways movement is meaningful to them (in both positive and negative ways), it also serves three other purposes. First, by sharing their autobiographies with peers it opens them up to the idea that there are diverse stories within their class. This awakening helps them recognize the potential diversity of experience in their own future classes. Second, the assignment provides us with a 'window' into who our PSTs are, the nature of their relationship with movement and, most importantly, a foundation on which to begin constructing an understanding of meaningful experiences. Third, it aligns with the pedagogical principle of supporting *reflection* on the meaningfulness of PE (Ní Chróinín et al., 2018) as we carve out time for PSTs to think about their own experiences, and those of others.

A framework for future teachers' professional growth

The Deweyan conceptualization of professional development (Armour et al., 2017) that forms part of our teaching philosophy aligns well with

Meaningful PE and helps provide a framework to create experiences that support engagement with the features and embed reflection (Ní Chróinín et al., 2018).

The first part of this framework, *acknowledge complex learning processes*, was included in the description of the autobiographical inquiry assignment. By learning about our PSTs' lives and having them learn about each other, we are able to recognize and act upon the fact that learning is complex – as are the learners who are engaged in learning. Usually, the first activities we do in the gym consist of cooperative games that are focused on *fun* and *social interaction*. These simple games also demonstrate the complexity of learning in PE due to the ways that there is interplay between the physical, cognitive, affective, and behavioural learning domains. For example, PSTs collaborate (affective) to solve a problem (cognitive) based on a movement task (physical). The PSTs' experience of playing these games is then used to elicit a discussion on the *features* of Meaningful PE as the students identify the presence or absence of the features through their personal and collective experiences (*reflection*). In this way, we are able to use the features to guide and analyze their experiences (Ní Chróinín et al., 2018).

The second part of the framework, *prioritize context and challenge*, is partially realized in the fact that we are coming to our PSTs in *their communities*. This requires us to learn about their specific context and how it impacts them – where they live, where they teach, and where they learn. In Fort McMurray, Doug uses community resources and takes PSTs outside to local parks and playgrounds to see what is possible, therefore modelling how to make movement experiences *personally relevant*. In Spring 2019, Jodi's class at Slave Lake experienced a traumatic encounter as forest fires threatened the town and it was evacuated. As a result, all PSTs were moved to Edmonton, housed at the University, and Jodi taught on campus. She drew on the features of *personal relevance* and *social interaction* to make PSTs feel welcome, acknowledge the trauma, and build learning experiences that embraced their challenges and new context. Jodi framed her learning activities using the features so that PSTs could experience and *reflect* on their experiences.

The third part of the framework is keeping classes *praxis-focused* (intersecting theory and practice). We do this in a number of ways. For example, when we introduce *motor competence* and *challenge,* we begin with student-centred, experiential tasks designed to bring theories of child development and motivation to life. A gymnastics activity, such as creating themed obstacle courses to encourage development in a dominant movement pattern, allows PSTs *autonomy* to explore theory and practice together. Our lesson planning assignment begins with establishing what 'good' lessons in

PE look and feel like in practice, and we explore the educational and pedagogical theories behind such lessons. The same planning assignment also includes acknowledging explicit elements of the features of Meaningful PE. Each student adapts their particular emphasis in the assignment based on personal teaching and community contexts (rural, urban, elementary, secondary, etc.).

The final part of the framework, *nurture career long growth*, is to us, a natural extension of the purpose of the course. We only have 39 hours of class time with PSTs. Teaching them everything they need to know about teaching PE would be impossible, which means our main goal is to develop lifelong learners. Therefore, we begin with moving PSTs to *value* PE as part of a whole child approach to education. Meaningful PE plays a distinct role here, as when PSTs come to experience meaningfulness as a participant or learner they can then assign value to those experiences. The next step is for them to develop an *identity* as a teacher of PE. This process is especially important for those PSTs who have had mis-educative experiences in PE and physical activity as well as for those who do identify as 'sporty' or 'athletes' (as more of our secondary PE students tend to do). It is critical for primary/elementary generalists to see themselves as teachers of PE; otherwise good teaching practice seems to end at the gym doors in our teacher education programs. Once our PSTs come to value PE and identify themselves as being able to teach it, we believe it is then that we can introduce pedagogy and tap into motivation for continuous professional development over what we hope will be a long career.

The Winter Count assignment

Our final example is our concluding assignment, which is called the *Winter Count*. According to Narcisse Blood (2020), who is a coordinator of Kainah Studies at Red Crow College: 'Winter count is a way of reckoning time, a tribal calendar of history. A long-ago person sat down to record the memorable events from a round of seasons on a tanned buffalo hide' (Reckoning Time Section, para. 1). In his book accounting the history of the Blackfoot people, Raczka (1979) stated:

> The winter count is an important record. Not only does it give us a historical record of the Blackfeet people greater than that previously recorded, but also an insight into these events. The memories of those elders still living have been added to the events as well as those of past researchers. It was the feelings of people that started this record, and they should be carried with it.
>
> (p. 5)

Even though it is a final assignment for the course, in keeping with the spirit of a historical Winter Count, it begins on day one. In these northern and rural programs, we often follow a unique schedule that allows the instructor to be in the community for a longer period of time. For example, rather than condense all program events into an intensive experience, Doug flew up to Fort McMurray six times in a term and would teach for an afternoon, stay overnight, teach the following morning, and then fly home. This meant that PSTs were given time to **reflect** on their experience, questions, and learning at the end of each session using the reflection tool (Figure 8.1).

By the end of the course, they have had 12 opportunities (one afternoon class and one morning class for each of Doug's trips) to reflect. As part of the Winter Count assignment, they are required to create 12 'symbols' that represent their learning and display them using a medium of their choosing (PPT, poster, or more creative versions such as dream catchers and faux buffalo hides). Each symbol must also be accompanied with a paragraph explaining the rationale for the symbol as well as the learning it represents. In our experience, this assignment leads to deep **reflection** for

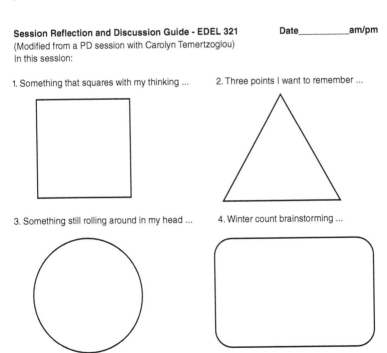

Figure 8.1 Reflection tool

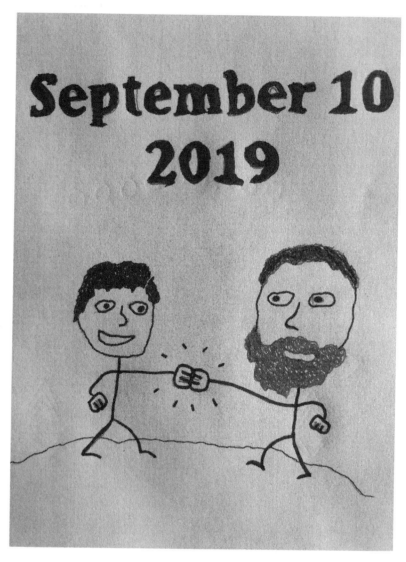

Figure 8.2 Winter Count

our PSTs and results in a richer display of learning than a final exam could ever replicate.

Figure 8.2 is a recreation of an example of a PST's Winter Count symbol. The September 10 symbol shows two stick figures shaking hands. The PST wrote:

For our first class, my symbol depicts me and Doug shaking hands. I remember during this first class, Doug made it apparent that we were all valued as individuals and that he wanted to interact with each and every one of us to ensure he would remember all of our names early on in the semester. This approach of an instructor is unfortunately the first I have come across in my journey as a student, therefore I will be sure to implement it in my teaching environment in my future as an educator! This initial class did not set the tone of the semester feeling like a chore, it fostered a safe and enjoyable environment that everyone could learn together in whilst feeling comfortable and valued.

The Winter Count also acts as a reflection tool for us as instructors. It provides insights into what students actually learned from each section of the class as opposed to what we had *hoped* they learned. Looking for dissonance or accordance to our purposes and plans for each of the 12 sessions helps us to be continually learning and tweaking our classes.

Previously in the 'How' section, we shared that we leaned on the feature of *social interaction* to set up a safe and supportive environment for our classes right from the start. The Winter Count example demonstrates the value of our strategy and the importance of modeling pedagogies that support Meaningful PE.

Concluding reflection

Our biggest takeaway from our experiences thus far is the importance of getting to know our students, valuing them as learners, and respecting them as individuals with unique and varied experiences (Dewey, 1938). This was especially important in rural and northern Canadian contexts as we needed to take the time to get to know and understand the community, the people, and their cultures. As such, we tended to focus more on the features of *social interaction, personal relevance,* and *fun* – within a 'bubble' of *joy (delight)*. We prioritized these features as a way into the hearts and minds of our PSTs that allowed us to create – together – a safe space to learn, play, and grow in our conception of Meaningful PE. It's not that we didn't include activities with *'just right' challenges* or build some capacities to understand and develop *motor competence*. It's just that these features were not as essential to the foregrounding of the culture we were trying to create and the environment we were trying to provide.

The ethos of Meaningful PE is, by its very nature, student-centred, which means that the focus of our class is the PST experience. Like Kretchmar (2008), we believe that by focusing on meaningful experiences, we can better shape and contextualize decisions about content, pedagogy, assessment, and curriculum, which can change the very culture of the class. PSTs feel valued and part of an educational community – one that is striving towards meaningfulness in physical education and teaching. Consider the following email from a PST in our program:

> I just wanted to say how much I truly appreciated your class. I had a physical education class last winter, the instructor was an incredible person, but there were some fellow students that made me feel embarrassed and ashamed. I don't like missing classes and so I showed up anyway, but there were times where I'd have to sit out or not engage in an activity, and I dreaded every moment of it because of them. I was so nervous coming to your class for the first time, but every class I got more and more comfortable. You set the tone right off the bat and it made for a space that I felt I fit into. You cannot imagine the impact that had on me personally and the ways through which it will positively benefit me in my own teaching practise. I hope to be able to make my students feel, even partially, the way you made me feel throughout this course!

A teaching vision for meaningfulness and joy honours and respects both the individual PST and the class as a collective, and the rights of both to experience these things in our course and their future teaching. Moving forward, we will continue to embed meaningfulness and joy into our teacher education classes and search for ways to improve the PST experience. Currently, the following four thoughts help guide how we plan to use Meaningful PE now and in the near future:

1   *Move away from a reliance on the features of meaningful experiences to embrace PSTs' own constructions of meaningfulness.* We want to be more organic in the way meaningfulness is introduced in our classes and therefore want to engage PSTs in considering their own conceptualizations of constructing meaning through movement. Perhaps there are limitations placed on creativity and imagination if we begin with a set idea of six features – let's see what else is out there!

2   *Highlight Dewey's (1938) theory of experience more clearly and explicitly through assignments designed to highlight joy and meaningfulness, while also recognizing the power of reflection in identifying mis-educative experiences.* Given that we only have 39 hours in which to teach our PSTs, it is tempting to relegate reflection and authentic engagement with experience to an out of class assignment or task. We want to make sure we create space both outside and inside the class time we are provided. As such, we model the importance of PSTs doing the same for their future students.

3   *Make Meaningful PE more explicit in the class structures (course out-lines, assignments, reflections) while also honouring the implicit emergence of meaningfulness.* To be blunt, we feel that the line between explicit and implicit is a knife edge – but it is an edge we must walk! While we know that embedding Meaningful PE in the very structure of our course is important, in some ways we do not want to 'give things away' too early and stifle the creativity and imagination that can result in implicit revelations and awakenings (see #1 of this list). We will keep wrestling with this thought and get back to you. . . .

4   *Seek ways for our PSTs to develop visions, ideas, plans, and implementation strategies for Meaningful PE that are contextual and student (K-12) focused.* We want to explore ideas on how to shift PSTs from thinking and acting on Meaningful PE like students to thinking and acting like teachers. One of the ways we could pursue this goal is to provide in-class teaching experiences with actual students so that PSTs can grapple with how to take their learning about meaningfulness into their future classes with their future students. Providing such an experience, with appropriate reflection time and tools, could be invaluable.

References

Armour, K., Quennerstedt, M., Chambers, F., & Makopoulo, K. (2017). What is 'effective' CPD for contemporary physical education teachers? A Deweyan framework. *Sport, Education and Society, 22,* 799–811.

Blood, N. (2020, February 15). *Since time immemorial.* Trailtribes. Retrieved from https://trailtribes.org/greatfalls/since-time-immemorial.htm

Dewey, J. (1938). *Experience in education.* New York, NY: Collier MacMillan Publishers.

Gleddie, D. L., Hickson, C., & Bradford, B. (2018). *Physical education for elementary school teachers: Foundations of a physical literacy journey.* Victoria, BC: Ripon Publishing.

Kretchmar, R. S. (2000). Movement subcultures: Sites for meaning. *Journal of Physical Education, Recreation and Dance, 71*(5), 19–25.

Kretchmar, R. S. (2005). Teaching games for understanding and the delights of human activity. In L. Griffin & J. Butler (Eds.), *Teaching games for understanding: Theory, research, and practice* (pp. 199–212). Champaign, IL: Human Kinetics.

Kretchmar, R. S. (2008). The increasing utility of elementary school physical education: A mixed blessing and unique challenge. *The Elementary School Journal, 108,* 161–170.

Ní Chróinín, D., Beni, S., Fletcher, T., Griffin, C., & Price, C. (2019). Using meaningful experiences as a vision for physical education teaching and teacher education practice. *Physical Education and Sport Pedagogy, 24,* 598–614.

Ní Chróinín, D., Fletcher, T., & O'Sullivan, M. (2018). Pedagogical principles of learning to teach meaningful physical education. *Physical Education and Sport Pedagogy, 23*, 117–133.

Raczka, P. M. (1979). *Winter count: A history of the Blackfoot people.* Calgary, AB: Friesen Printers.

University of Alberta. (2020a). *Aboriginal teacher education program.* Retrieved from www.ualberta.ca/aboriginal-teacher-education-program

University of Alberta. (2020b). *Collaborative program.* Retrieved from www.ualberta.ca/education/programs/undergraduate-programs/collaborative-off-campus-degree

Wilson, S. (1995). Honoring spiritual knowledge and memory comes before knowledge. *Canadian Journal of Native Education, 21*(Suppl.), 61–69.

Part IV

Moving forward with Meaningful Physical Education

9   Reflections on and possibilities for Meaningful Physical Education

Mary O'Sullivan, with Michelle Alberts,
Laura Boudens, Nadeen Halls,
Autumn Nesdoly and Ty Riddick

From the editors

In this final chapter we invited several people to contribute based on their exposure to and familiarity with Meaningful PE. Our invitation extended to people with various backgrounds and interests in PE: Michelle, Laura, Nadeen, and Ty teach PE in schools, Autumn is a graduate student with interests in youth sport and Indigeneity, and Mary is Professor Emeritus in physical education teacher education (PETE).

The chapter is divided into two main sections. In the first section, Michelle, Laura, and Nadeen contribute pedagogical case studies based on their learning as part of a graduate course on Meaningful Physical Education at the University of Alberta. Much like the pedagogical cases on the Meaningful PE website, these cases combine both real and imagined scenarios, and serve as possibilities for how they and other teachers (i.e., readers) might use ideas from Meaningful PE in schools and classrooms. In the second section, Ty, Autumn, and Mary offer reflective commentaries based on their interpretations of the chapters in the text and other experiences they have had with Meaningful PE. Ty and Autumn were both students in the graduate course at University of Alberta, and Mary was an influential member of the research team in the first three years of the LAMPE project.

Pedagogical case 1: Meaningful PE in a social dance unit, by Michelle Alberts

I find great joy in teaching social dance to students; however, I am aware that many students enter this unit with negative previous experiences that may impact how they perceive their upcoming experience. Meaningful PE offers a way to challenge those experiences by placing students' voices at the centre of my decision-making.

I began the unit with a class discussion where I outlined expectations and asked students to use their mobile devices to complete an anonymous 'poll everywhere' question where they described their previous experiences in social dance. This platform sends responses into a forum where students can see and reflect on other anonymous responses from their peers. I noticed how students shared commonalities in many responses. Many responses involved experiences of social anxiety, comparisons, self-image, lack of quality instruction, lack of meaning, and lack of a safe learning environment provided by the teacher.

Following the 'poll everywhere' activity, I asked questions that focused on how students might find dance meaningful, such as: 'Where may you engage in moments of social dance throughout your lives?' Students shared answers such as: 'weddings, birthdays, anniversaries, etc.'. These answers stimulated discussion and led to the next question: 'Why do you think some adults refrain from engaging in aspects of social dance at these types of events?' Students shared answers such as: 'They are self-conscious, or they don't know how. Perhaps a fear of rejection or ridicule'. Through discussion of potential worries and deterrents, the class seemed at ease before beginning the movement tasks in the unit. I had not previously taken the time to tap into **student voice** with this level of detail and openness, which may have been a reason why many students struggled to find a connection with and the relevance of dance in their own lives.

I provided a brief description of several genres of dance through verbal instruction and video. Students selected individualized (e.g., line dances or interpretive choreography), partner (e.g., two-step, polka, jive) or group dances (e.g., group choreography) to participate in. By providing students **choice**, they may find their experience more meaningful because they have some ownership in the process. Students were encouraged to sign up for which genre they felt most compelled to participate in or learn more about. Once students were all signed up, they were grouped together for one week according to their preferences.

Due to the different groups and their preferences I had to use multiple strategies to teach, including: direct instruction, printed instructions, YouTube videos, QR codes, and peer instruction (inviting students with dance experience to volunteer). Depending on which group students chose to participate in, they were given modifications and various levels of **challenge** to choose from. Students were also invited to create their own partner or group dance, which provided opportunities for **social interactions** among their peers. At the end of class, students were provided with instructions for the next class and were asked to complete an exit slip about their experiences so far, which asked them to share two positive experiences and one area for improvement for tomorrow. This exit slip allowed for **reflection** and communication among the class and helped me adjust my approach based on students' needs and interests.

I observed positive changes in the attitude of many students and the levels of participation in comparison to previous classes. I believe this was mostly due to providing choice and levels of optimal challenge. But beyond my observations, I made sure to individually connect with students about their experiences. Many said things like: 'It wasn't as bad as I thought it would be'; however, some said the dance unit is just not for them. I commended these students for their honesty and for sticking with something that was perhaps not their favourite activity. I used these responses to discuss how 'not quitting something' transferred to authentic experiences inside and outside of school (*personally relevant learning*). Following this discussion, I noticed a shift in the thinking of some students.

As a final point of feedback, students assessed their overall experience and competency levels. Many responded with: 'thumbs up' and 'thumbs sideways'. This stimulated my thinking about this unit in the future. Perhaps students could provide evidence of how they engage in social dance in their lives (e.g., at social events) or they could organize social dance opportunities for other students in the school. More teachers could be invited to integrate dance into other subjects. For example, a language arts teacher could invite students to create an interpretive dance to express the theme of a short story or novel.

Several weeks after concluding the social dance unit, I organized a flash-mob to celebrate the holiday season while building school culture and spreading the joy of dance. To my surprise, over fifty students participated, including many who completed the social dance unit. Later in the year at a school dance, a student requested a song for a line dance that was previously taught in the social dance unit, and many students joined to dance with one another, including me!

Pedagogical case 2: Meaningful PE in a running unit, by Laura Boudens

One of the first units I teach each year is 'cross-country running'. Cross-country running figures prominently at my school, and we have a long and proud record of outstanding performance. My school is located in a rural setting and there are lots of outdoor spaces I can access with my classes. Most classes in this unit involve students heading outside to run on the beautiful trails. This was a three-week long unit which culminated with a K-6 cross-country race, which was a long-standing event at the school.

When I think back to how I first taught this unit, it was not inclusive. Students were readily labeled: athletic, not good at PE, strong/weak runners, in/out of shape, proud, embarrassed, go-getters, or slackers. I stood with the stopwatch recording students' times at the finish line. Lessons felt rushed and slower runners had less time to play ultimate Frisbee with their peers. We gave awards to the top six runners in each grade and all students' race times were posted in the hallway for at least two weeks following the unit. I saw some students throw their participation ribbons in the garbage, while others pinned them to their shirts.

I highly value the development of an inclusive classroom community, and upon reflection, it was clear that this was lacking in the cross-country and ultimate Frisbee unit. Things had to change, but I realized this would take time. I observed and asked questions, particularly in order to get student feedback to gauge their feelings (*student voice*). Sure enough, cross-country running was their least favourite unit of Term 1. The results facilitated open discussion in the PE department. If the goal of our program was to encourage students to enjoy being active, our current approach was not serving that purpose.

The following year we began looking at ways we could maintain high expectations while being more inclusive and *fun*. This led us to change the introductory unit to one of adventure challenges, with an aim to create a safe space for students. We then followed this introductory unit with our cross-country running unit, albeit with a more interactive and inclusive approach. For example, running buddies were chosen by students to enable positive *interaction with peers* to support making PE more meaningful. There was also a major shift away from timing students regularly. We now offered a variety of running routes to vary distance options for students, aiming to facilitate *choice* and *challenge* for students. We created a scavenger hunt, bringing more *fun* and *social interaction* into the unit.

One year later and more changes have been made to prioritize meaningfulness in the cross-country unit. The unit began with everyone walking the route together to ensure that no student felt like they couldn't keep up on the first day. *Goal-setting* was introduced, which encouraged regularly discussing objectives of the unit and highlighting how goals are different for each person. Students who wanted to improve their speed were given interval training challenges. Teachers no longer timed students; if students wanted to keep track of and improve their time, they were given the option to time themselves. Students who set a goal to walk less (hence, running more) were given trail markers to track their improvements. Students who wanted to run with a buddy or jog-walk while chatting with a friend could access a jog-walk training option and different trails.

It is vital to recognize how teacher actions impact student experiences and learning. To take this unit further, I feel there is a need for a whole school approach so we can discuss the scope and sequence of what cross-country running can look like. It will be important to discuss ways we can continue to keep cross-country running as a vibrant part of our school's culture and traditions, while also preventing negative experiences and supporting students to meet their optimal level of challenge. Encouraging student agency by supporting individualized goal-setting also helps to make learning more personally relevant to students. The teacher can then differentiate lessons to appeal to the various goals and competency levels.

If teachers know what experiences their students identify as meaningful, they can begin to plan accordingly. Continuing to seek student feedback, or utilizing a PE journal, can help teachers ensure students play an active role in lesson and unit planning. In this case, seeking student feedback on the cross-country running unit prompted teachers to re-evaluate plans and begin the process of making changes to the unit.

Pedagogical case 3: Meaningful PE in a scooter unit, by Nadeen Halls

I teach in a school with a highly diverse and complex student population. It includes many English Language Learners (ELL), refugees, Indigenous children, and students with special needs. To address the needs of our students, the school has a Well-being Professional Learning Community (PLC) and School Wellness Action Team. Our Well-being PLC meets every Friday afternoon, and we focus on trauma-informed practice and social and emotional learning, with specific attention to self-regulation. For this reason, in the development of PE programming, I am always looking for opportunities to address, develop, and support self-regulation strategies to align with the work of other teachers at the school while maintaining a vision of supporting and encouraging students to become active for life.

When I began teaching at my school I would introduce a game. The game would quickly erupt into conflict, or the instructions for the game proved to be too complex. I quickly recognized that many of my students needed support with social-emotional skill building and thrived when the activities were simplified and scaffolded. I saw a video of a teacher in my district who was given special permission to offer skateboarding for students with complex backgrounds to support them in pursuit of their learning goals. After watching the video, I was inspired to nudge forward with what was allowable and manageable within our school context. Skateboarding is prohibited in our district, so I thought that some scooters (push or kick scooters) might have a similar effect. I asked around to some friends who had kids and then posted on a community social media page. Slowly we built up our scooter collection with donations on my doorstep and gifts from outside partnerships.

The challenge then was to not only consider the work around self-regulation but also about how to make scootering experiences meaningful to students. Considering the *features* of Meaningful PE helped identify areas that were supporting meaningfulness and those that warranted further attention.

> *Personally relevant learning:* Students who naturally navigated themselves towards our scooters were some of my most complex students. This included those with more challenging behaviours or some who had experienced significant trauma. Some asked to ride scooters during recess or other times during the day; some of their teachers observed that the scooters were effective in helping many students self-regulate.

> *Social interaction:* Although we now use scooters regularly, there have been some significant changes in the ability of some of my students to interact with others. At skate and scooter parks, there is a good deal of etiquette involved. There is a need to take turns and share equipment. Helmets must be worn, which encourages personal responsibility and safety. One needs to be aware of others: our tarmac is only just large enough to navigate a safe speed. They also need to avoid the areas where hockey and basketball nets are set up and the school's back doors where teachers and students come and go. They also need to be willing to help someone who has a crash. These can be painful but encourage empathy. Crashing also encourages monitoring their own safety to avoid further crashes. Social capital has increased significantly for some students who did not always feel included.

> *Fun:* There is a lot of the usual feedback in terms of smiles, laughter, squeals of joy, and comments such as 'Scooters are fun, Miss!' But now I pause and take the time to ask why they are fun. They tell me they feel free when they can go fast, they love the challenge of trying new tricks, they can race their friends, and they can 'go around the corner'. Going around the corner is where the smooth tarmac is. I ask them to promise to not go too far and be safe coming back. This adds to the trust that we have built and they like that.

> *Motor competence and challenge:* Students who had no previous exposure to scooters were initially tentative but now many have gained confidence and experiment with and/or master tricks. Peer instruction is amazing as I see many ELL students trying to explain how to do a trick in English! These interactions are what make it all very worth the effort.

I see many ways in which the features of Meaningful PE help to assess the value of the scooter unit for the students. As my own confidence and comfort in their participation grows, I now start to revisit my initial thoughts on how I could access skateboarding for my students because they have expressed an interest in progressing from scooters to skateboards and have demonstrated so much growth with scooters. A successful process will support student growth and could result in teachers and students exploring these as not only acceptable activities but ones that support student well-being and thriving.

A PE teacher's commentary on Meaningful PE by, Ty Riddick

Joe loves nothing more than to pull on his hiking boots and start his way up a mountain trail. He finds the fresh mountain air rejuvenating and the challenge of the climb rewarding. During the week, Joe participates in an adult basketball league, and although he does not shoot it like he used to, he enjoys spending time with his friends. Joe has had a number of meaningful experiences that have allowed him to turn some of his environments into his own personal playgrounds. But how has Joe reached this point? From an educator's perspective, how many meaningful experiences are needed for students to, like Joe, approach these environments with 'a sense of excitement, joy, and adventure rather than dread or fear'? (Ch 1, this volume).

These questions are, of course, somewhat rhetorical and would be unrealistic to attempt to quantify. Yet, they are also thought-provoking and worthy of consideration. Throughout the book, several experienced educators have shared their introspective journey of how the Meaningful PE approach came to take its place at the core of their personal teaching philosophies and practices. However, as I continue to engage in a similar journey, I cannot help but wonder whether devoting my personal practice to Meaningful PE is enough to produce the intended outcome of students pursuing delightful experiences outside of the school day. Working with the features of Meaningful PE can be challenging due to their personalized and interrelated nature. In the same way, rushing through content to cover curriculum standards does not necessarily result in optimal learning outcomes – emphasizing the features of meaningful experience and including reflective tasks does not necessarily result in a meaningful experience for every student in every lesson or unit. Each student may place different values on different features, and thus meaningful experiences need to be unearthed by teacher and student together, which often takes patient nurturing. Fortunately, for teachers such as Milena Trojanovic (Chapter 3) who teach in a smaller department, there are multiple opportunities to share this responsibility for meaningful experience with students as they progress through multiple grade levels. However, in other educational contexts, a teacher who places an emphasis on Meaningful PE may only teach a student for a single grade, potentially resulting in a fairly limited number of opportunities for this patient nurturing to occur. So again, I wonder: Is my individual teaching philosophy 'enough'?

While I do not wish to diminish the significant impact that a single teacher can have on the lives of young people, when it comes to meaningful experiences for students, my prevailing sense has come to be that the responsibility needs to be shared between students and all the physical educators that a student will be taught by at their school. Of course, this is easier said than done. In our department's journey, one of the first tasks critical to this endeavour was understanding our own value-orientations as well as those of our colleagues. Using Kretchmar's (2008) article we placed ourselves on a continuum from health to joy-oriented and discussed which was deserving of priority in our context. Perhaps the more important task was to understand why and how each of us came to value these orientations. When we took the time to reflect and share our own movement experiences, the features of the Meaningful PE framework began to reveal themselves. Although each of us placed more value on certain features, the role these features played in our movement histories was undeniable, and thus the Meaningful PE framework began to become central in our planning, professional dialogue, and reflection. Over the span of two years, we experimented with a number of new approaches and shared new learning based on student feedback and reflection. At the end of the school year, inspired by the case studies on the LAMPE website (Chapter 6), we wrote our own case studies and submitted them as an advocacy piece to our administration so they could better understand this new pedagogical approach. Having gained the support of administration, these case studies served as an example of reflective practice and will become a part of a more flexible professional growth portfolio next school year that is responsive to the needs of specific departments in the school. With that in mind, I hope the educators reading this text are willing to start a dialogue within their own department and with administrators in order for Meaningful PE to be transformed from an individual teaching philosophy to the foundational core of their department and school's mission and vision.

A sport researcher's commentary on Meaningful PE, by Autumn Nesdoly

From my engagement with Meaningful PE, I believe it may be a useful tool to support meaningfulness in PE and sport settings. The knowledge and experiences that have been shared throughout this text only act to bolster this understanding. From my perspective, the Meaningful PE approach is well-positioned to support – rather than act in competition with – other initiatives (e.g., physical literacy, teaching games for understanding, positive youth development) in PE and sport settings. As such, more physical educators and coaches may be encouraged to adopt this framework into their own practice; better yet, many may begin to consider how facilitating Meaningful PE experiences is already a part of their instruction and/or vision for PE and sport.

I was recently involved in a project that explored the perspectives of physical literacy with Indigenous peoples. Upon reflection, it is clear that there is considerable overlap between how the collaborators (i.e., ten Indigenous coaches, educators, and youth mentors) described physical literacy and the framework of Meaningful PE. For instance, the collaborators discussed ideas of wisdom sharing; being mindful of teachings, culture, and spirituality as part of being active for life; youth-centred approaches and relational support (Nesdoly, Gleddie, & McHugh, 2020). As one example, the concept of wisdom sharing, defined as 'a process of sharing knowledge and history with Indigenous youth through picture and stories', was suggested to facilitate deep conversation with, and support critical observations by, youth (Nesdoly et al., 2020, p. 7). This aligns well with Dewey's (1938) suggestion to provide opportunities for individuals to reflect on their experiences to strengthen their understandings. More importantly, wisdom sharing relates to the feature of personally relevant learning as presented in Chapter 1. Thus, the Meaningful PE approach may be useful in facilitating physical literacy experiences amongst Indigenous youth. Educators and coaches should consider this when developing programs that aim to foster Meaningful PE and sport experiences.

By committing to a vision of meaningful experiences for learners in PE and sport, practitioners take on a student-centred approach that promotes opportunities for students to find delight and/or the joy of movement in PE and sport settings. Further, facilitating experiences that foster personally relevant learning may indeed support educators and coaches in their endeavours to develop transformative and socially responsive physical activity programming. Such programming may lead to a shift in how movement is viewed and experienced by *all* students. Several scholars have discussed the exclusive (rather than inclusive) learning climate that PE and sport traditionally involves; thus, the Meaningful PE approach may act as a solid foundation to act against the use of traditional practices in sport and PE settings and facilitate transformation in those systems. For these reasons, I think there is tremendous potential in using, researching, and developing meaningful experiences in both settings.

Learning and meaning in PE aligned to the times we live in, by Mary O'Sullivan

These COVID-19 times are challenging how people live their lives, causing us to change our behaviour in order to live safely with this virus. The public health advice to stay apart from, yet maintain (remotely) connections with family and friends is a grand challenge. We have seen increasing anxiety and stress levels, especially among the elderly, vulnerable and young people in society (United Nations Human Rights Commission, 2020). Restrictions on personal freedoms have given rise to substantive reflections about the meaning of life and how best to live our lives into the future. There has been increased interest in people decamping from cities to live in coastal and rural areas to raise their families, with technology allowing them to work remotely. The values of time with family, friends and friendship, nature, and being active outdoors have been heightened.

Worldwide, sporting activities stopped for several months and the impact was particularly acute for young people and their communities. The interactions with friends and coaches previously afforded by sport heightened recognition about the important role of sport in communities and young people's lives. The joy and pleasure of engaging in sport is presented as central to the social/emotional as well as physical development of young people, and efforts to get them back to school and playing sport are now key government priorities internationally.

The COVID-19 narrative shifted the focus on movement to its role in the social and emotional development of young people and living happy and fulfilling lives. It is presented as a key enabler of young people engaging with friends while challenging themselves on the running track, pitch, dance floor, or in the water. I contrast this with what was a more prominent demand for young people's engagement in moderate to high levels of physical activity for long-term health. The focus now is on safe and enjoyable physical activity engagement that respects the diversity of interests and talents of young people. I contend that in addressing these values, the future health outcomes of young people will be a by-product, not a focus.

I saw firsthand the excitement in reopening our local playing pitches for sport training following five months of closure in 2020 due to COVID-19. The joy of parents, young people, and coaches in these early mornings was palpable. The value of sport shifted to a clear recognition of its centrality to quality of life in the community and the flourishing of young people (Seligman, 2011). These are the values that LAMPE/Meaningful PE advocates in its approach to teaching and coaching sport and dance in school and community settings, and why the approach is truly well aligned for teaching and coaching in our times.

Meaningful PE characteristics inform pedagogical decisions bringing joy and relevance to young people

PE, as articulated through the key features of Meaningful PE, is ideally aligned to the zeitgeist of contemporary society and to sporting engagement, bringing challenge and pleasure to young people as they learn about who they are and what is important to them. Teachers who align with Meaningful PE seek to make pedagogical decisions that respect students' interests and talents and allow them opportunities to lead and learn while building sporting competence and friendships. The teachers in the case studies presented in this chapter provide guidance on how Meaningful PE can be used in teaching. They describe the pedagogical decisions they made (or would make) to promote more meaningful experiences in PE for their students. In her case study, Michelle Alberts hypothetically asked her students to provide anonymous descriptions of their experiences with social dance and used the responses as a basis for discussion about how the group experienced dance in the past. Informed by student exit slips from class, Michelle planned for student choice in selecting a type of dance genre they would be most comfortable with, noting these decisions allowed for greater engagement, comfort with the dance content, and enjoyment in learning. Similarly, Laura Boudens shows how her (hypothetical) pedagogical decision-making in adapting a running unit (e.g., no public posting of personal times and student engagement in 'just right' challenges by setting their own goals for running tasks) resulted in a more inclusive and enjoyable unit for students while still maintaining the school's vibrant cross-country running tradition. Nadeen Halls used features of Meaningful PE (motor competence, challenge, fun, social interaction, and personally relevant learning) to hypothetically plan for students' goal-setting for their engagement with tasks on scooters. She imagined the class engagement and enjoyment of the unit using this approach (given some students were fearful on this equipment at outset). These teachers show how the features of Meaningful PE might be used to inform their curricular planning and decision-making with positive results for students. Meaningful PE provided a structure for pedagogical decisions focused on helping young people to thrive in various movement playgrounds by building their confidence, leadership, and social capacity during these learning opportunities.

Competence, content, reflection, and the challenge for teacher educators

How then to best prepare teachers with these values and capacities to lead out on teaching with a Meaningful PE approach? A challenge for PE teacher educators is to facilitate pre-service teachers' learning to teach PE based on values that exemplify these philosophical ideals through using LAMPE. The teacher education challenge is most intense when planning for those who are learning to teach primary PE. In many countries, teachers of PE are generalists and their teacher education program prepares them to teach ten or more other subject areas within a two-year (graduate entry) or four-year undergraduate teacher education program. Irish teacher educator Maura Coulter noted (Chapter 7) a key challenge with LAMPE in that environment: battling to balance a focus on student voice and student reflection with a desire to help pre-service teachers learn to teach the many content strands of the PE curriculum framework. She said: 'I'm finding the reflection [by pre-service teachers] so worthwhile and necessary, and if we want [pre-service teachers] to do it with children, we should surely model it. But I am battling with losing content!' Teacher educators almost always want more time to cover the variety of subject matter activity strands (sports, movement forms) in PE. How to get a balance?

The words of the late Sir Ken Robinson (RIP 2020) are helpful in this respect. He suggests we use the current 'COVID education system' as an opportunity to cultivate children's diverse talents and interests by focusing on learning 'culture not content'. He encouraged opportunities for students to collaborate in learning and to demonstrate compassion and empathy for others in that process. He suggested that building such a culture will ensure that the outcomes (formal assessments of learning outcomes) would follow (Sandomir, 2020).

As teacher educators we provide pre-service teachers the opportunity to unpack their reasons for pedagogical practices and discuss how their own biographies of movement experiences impact their values and how their decisions as young teachers may (or may not) cultivate children's diverse talents and interests in the movement culture. This critical self-reflection and capacity for action is a core element of teacher education, and the characteristics of LAMPE allow a structure to interrogate these values while learning to teach. This approach to quality PE is not a panacea for good teaching. Rather it is a heuristic to consider what Meaningful PE is and how to support young people to engage and thrive in our movement cultures.

References

Dewey, J. (1938). *Experience and education.* New York, NY: Palgrave Macmillan.
Kretchmar, R. S. (2008). The increasing utility of elementary school physical education: A mixed blessing and unique challenge. *The Elementary School Journal, 108*, 161–170.

Nesdoly, A., Gleddie, D., & McHugh, T. L. F. (2020). An exploration of Indigenous peoples' perspectives of physical literacy. *Sport, Education and Society*, 1–14.

Sandomir, R. (2020, September 11). Robinson who preached creativity in teaching dies. *New York Times*. Retrieved from www.nytimes.com/2020/09/11/world/europe/ken-robinson-who-preached-creativity-in-teaching-dies-at-70.html

Seligman, M. E. P. (2011). *Flourish: A visionary new understanding of happiness and well-being*. New York, NY: Atria Books.

United Nations Human Rights Commission. (2020). *United nations committee on the rights of the child recommendations for protecting children in times of COVID*. Retrieved from https://tbinternet.ohchr.org/_layouts/15/treatybodyexternal/Download.aspx?Lang=en&symbolno=INT%2FCRC%2FSTA%2F9095

Index